THE PLACE WHERE A STORY ENDED - EXPANDED EDITION

HAMICE L CADAE

Copyright © 2021-2023 by Hamice L. Cadae

All rights reserved.

No part of this publication may be reproduced, distributed, or transmitted in any form or by any means, including photocopying, recording, information storage and retrieval systems, or other electronic or mechanical methods, without the prior written permission of the author, except in the case of brief quotations embodied in critical reviews and certain other noncommercial uses permitted by copyright law.

First Edition: September 2021

Expanded Edition: September 2023

Cover photography by iStock.com/shin001.

ISBN: 978-1-7378496-2-9

EMAIL: hcadae@gmail.com

This book is dedicated to MEVS

Forrest Fenn.
Who?
A man. A plan.

What?

The Thrill of the Chase.
A book. A poem. Twenty-four lines.
Treasures.
A secret location.

What does it all mean?

Indulgence.
New life from old growth
Was the fulfillment of an oath.
O'er his bed we will plant the wild rose.
Time to sleep, a last repose.

Contents

Preface xi
Introduction xv

FENNOLOGY 1

Part I
Game Theory

IT'S ABOUT TIME 9
SHALL WE PLAY A GAME? 12
THE GAME DESIGNER 15
THE GOLDILOCKS ZONE 19
THE TARGET AUDIENCE 23
THE PLAYING FIELD 27
THE RULEBOOKS 31
POSSIBILITIES AND PROBABILITIES 34
THE REFEREE 38
CONSTANT AS THE NORTHERN STAR 43
LOST IN TRANSLATION 46
THROUGH THE LOOKING GLASS 51
TALL TALES & FLIGHTS OF FANCY 54
FINITE AND INFINITE GAMES 58

Part II
Chaos Theory

THE GAME'S AFOOT 63
TRUST THE PROCESS 80
THERE'S NO PLACE LIKE HOME 83
THAT'S MY REFRAIN 88
AT AN IMPASSE 90
THE LITTLE GIRL FROM INDIA 93
A RIVER RUNS THROUGH IT 96
FLAMING FLOWERS THAT BRIGHTLY BLAZE 102
MY SECRET WHERE 106
CONFIDENCE IN A MAVERICK 110

TEA WITH OLGA	113
THE WIZARD OF OZ	117
THE CALUMET OF THE COTEAU	125
PIONEERS OF A DIFFERENT SORT	129
A KEY POINT	134
MYSTIC MISDIRECTION	137
I LEARNED THE TRUTH AT SEVENTEEN	139
X MARKS THE SPOT	146
THE OMEGA MAN	149
TO BOLDLY GO	152

Part III
Consilience

WHERE SOMEONE HAS GONE BEFORE	157
THE FALSE BLAZE	161
PURSUING IT WITH EAGER FEET	165
THE PLACE WHERE A STORY ENDED	168
THE CATCHER IN THE RYE	171
TARRY SCANT WITH MARVEL GAZE	173
INDULGENCE	175
METHOD IN THE MADNESS	177
NAVIGATIONAL NUPTIALS	180
THE BIG PICTURE	184
THE THRILL OF THE CHASE	187
BULLSEYE	190
ORDER FROM CHAOS	193
THE BIP THEORY	196
A SOUND SOLUTION	198
FLY ME TO THE MOON	202
BE PREPARED	205
THERE AND BACK AGAIN	208
FOR WHOM THE BELL TOLLS	214
MY WAR FOR ME	216

Part IV
Appendices

IT'S DANGEROUS TO GO ALONE	219
ANATOMY OF A HINT	223
YELLOWSTONE	225

IT'S NOT EASY BEING GREEN	227
HOLES	229
CLARK GABLE	231
THE ROSETTA STONE	233
DIZZY DEAN	236
FORGOTTEN	238
*	238
Bibliography	241
Epilogue	246
Acknowledgments	249
Suggested Reading	259
About the Author	263

Preface

For over a decade, a treasure chest filled with gold, jewels, and antique collectibles lay concealed amidst the vast expanse of the Rocky Mountains, a testament to the imagination and ingenuity of Forrest Fenn, a wealthy and eccentric former art dealer. The treasure chest, concealed by Fenn between 2009 and 2010, had been waiting patiently for someone to find it.

An estimated 300,000 searchers, fueled by passionate determination, sought the answer to a decade-old riddle created by Fenn. The saga of the treasure was immortalized in Fenn's memoir, *The Thrill of the Chase*. Within its pages was a poem, and within that poem, nine cryptic clues. The challenge was straightforward: decipher the poem, find the chest, and claim its riches. On June 6, 2020, Fenn announced that someone had done just that.

In the months after Fenn's announcement, veteran treasure hunters awaited details of the deed. Eager for Fenn's explanation of the 24-line poem they had tirelessly attempted to decode, they were met with silence. As it became clear that an explanation might never come, feelings of depression, anger, and angst grew among the searchers.

"This could not be the end of it. There was no feeling of closure at all, no sense of completeness. It was disappointing." Those words, a virtual prophecy from the author of the treasure hunt himself, were now felt by searchers the world over.

I waited with everyone else. The difference was that I knew the solution to the poem. I knew the story, but it wasn't my story, so I waited for someone else to tell it. And, I waited. And, I waited. Along with every other searcher, I waited.

And then, on September 7, 2020, two weeks after his 90th birthday, Forrest Fenn passed away. I had neither met nor spoken with Mr. Fenn. I sent him a few emails, but he never replied. Since he was receiving hundreds of emails per day, I figured he never saw mine. Although he had no idea who I was or that I even existed, I felt we knew each other just the same. Forrest was my fishing buddy, critiquing my technique in silence and furrowing his brow in disgust as I put bait on a hook.

Upon hearing the news of Forrest's passing, I shut down. The thrill of the chase had come to an end. Losing the race to the chest was disappointing, but I soon got over it. Forrest's passing left me empty, something I did not expect. I didn't care about the chase anymore and tried to find anything else to occupy my mind.

When I resurfaced several months later, searchers were still waiting for a story that would never be told. No, that's not accurate. They were waiting for the last chapter of a book they had grown to love. They already knew most of the story; the one thing missing was the climax—the part where all the pieces are tied together at the end.

A strangely insidious something began to gnaw on me. Two others knew the secret: one of them had died, the other wasn't talking, and the reasons given for the silence seemed specious. Many people were starting to question the legitimacy of everything Forrest had said and done.

Although Forrest did not seem concerned about his legacy, I find it unacceptable that his legacy is being tarnished and that the legitimacy of *The Thrill of the Chase* is being questioned when I can settle those questions. Forrest meant for his treasure hunt to give people hope, get them back out into nature, and maybe tell a story Forrest wanted to tell. It accomplished those first two objectives many times over, and I can do something about the third.

I now find myself in the unique position of being the only person left who can "safely" finish Forrest's story. If there are legitimate reasons for the silence, my words can be disavowed, deniability can be maintained, and the official narrative can continue. I'll even help with that right now.

Everything in this book is only my opinion.

According to the official narrative, I am wrong about everything. Everything contained in this book is incorrect, and my answer to Forrest's puzzle is not even in the correct state. Why then, since my interpretation is supposedly wrong, did I write this book, and why should you bother to read it?

It may seem that, without the treasure chest as confirmation, it is impossible to prove whether my interpretation of Forrest's poem is correct. In the strictest sense, this is true. It is possible, however, to provide an explanation so compelling that the majority will cast aside everything they thought they knew and exclaim, "Why didn't I think of that?" It is possible to provide such overwhelming evidence that people would not believe me were I to renounce my own solution.

This book weaves together all the loose ends into a cohesive last chapter of Forrest's *Thrill of the Chase*, and in so doing, it reveals the solution to the poem and story hidden within. I am confident that searchers will find closure within these pages and be satisfied in their hearts that they, at last, have the answers they sought.

Now, dive into a story that transcends the details of Forrest's enigma, appealing to anyone who loves the timeless allure of adventure, the thrill of a good mystery, and the joy of untangling a world-class riddle. Whether you're a seasoned treasure hunter or new to the saga, these pages promise a tale of intrigue that resonates with all curious souls.

Introduction

I first heard about Forrest Fenn and *The Thrill of the Chase* in late summer 2018. I received a short email that said, "Hey, look at this. You interested?" The email's author was always trying to instigate some form of mischief, so my guard was already up.

A man named Forrest Fenn started a treasure hunt back in 2010. According to Forrest, he placed over 20 pounds of gold, plus some jewels and artifacts, in a bronze treasure chest and hid it somewhere in the Rocky Mountains north of Santa Fe.

Okay, I thought. A treasure hunt looks interesting, but in all likelihood, it was a scam. As a service to the author of the email, I would prove it was a scam. The first order of business then was to investigate this Forrest Fenn character.

For the next week, I watched every video and listened to every radio interview I could find about Forrest Fenn. I paid particular attention to the videos so that I might scrutinize Forrest's expressions. I was not looking for the treasure; I was looking for signs of deception. I didn't see any, not at first. He seemed sincere. Everyone who knew Forrest vouched for him. "If Forrest said he hid it, he hid it," they insisted. Many of these people are famous in their own right and had no need to pander to Forrest.

As one of Santa Fe's premier art gallery owners between 1972 and 1988, Forrest had the means to pull off such an elaborate caper. The value of the items in the chest looked to be worth about one million dollars, not counting a collector's premium. With the amount of money the Fenn Galleries made with Forrest at the helm, he could afford to be a bit eccentric.

Forrest said he got the idea to hide the chest after being diagnosed with kidney cancer in 1988. Sometime later, Ralph Lauren, a friend of Forrest's, tried to persuade him to sell a prized artifact. Forrest said the item was not for sale. Ralph said, "You have so many, and you can't take them with you." Forrest replied, "Then I'm not going."

Later that night, Forrest thought, "Who says I can't take it with me? If I'm going to die from cancer, I'm going to take some stuff with me." So Forrest purchased an antique bronze chest and filled it with gold, jewels, and a few favorite mementos. Forrest planned to sneak away to a special location he had in mind and, with his last gasping breath, fling himself on top of the treasure chest and let his bones go back to the earth.

But then Forrest got better. Still, he said, "I told myself just because I got well doesn't mean I could not hide the treasure chest anyway." And the idea for the treasure hunt and *The Thrill of the Chase* was born.

Forrest had a roguish charm; the way he told his story was captivating and drew you into his world. But I wasn't interested in being captivated. I was interested in finding signs of deception, and I sensed deception in Forrest's story. He was hiding something, but what? The reason. I was not sold on Forrest's quirky and playful tale about taking it with him.

Forrest talked a great deal about people being forgotten: "Look at me, I'm somebody; please don't forget." Legacy. That was a more probable reason, but coming out and saying so could have the opposite of the desired effect. I sensed deception about the reason but not about the act. "I really did hide a treasure chest, but I'm not going to tell you why I did so" was the message being sent. All right then, Forrest, keep your secrets.

Whatever the reason, whether lark, legacy, or something else, Forrest's hiding a bronze box filled with goodies and then daring people to find it not only didn't seem farfetched, it seemed appropriate. Proving Forrest Fenn a fraud was not as easy as I thought it would be.

Still, the world is filled with rich people who want more. Although the poem was available for free online, any serious treasure searcher would buy Forrest's book. That was the scam then—put a real treasure out there, but get your money back and more with book sales. I don't know about the legalities of that, but Forrest took steps to ensure that wasn't even a question. Forrest paid for the publishing and printing costs for the first thousand books and then donated all of those books plus reprint rights to a local bookstore with the stipulation that they set aside 10% of the gross sales for a fund to help those with cancer. Forrest didn't make a dime from the sales of *The Thrill of the Chase*. Maybe this wasn't a scam after all.

One thing that continued to bother me was that it had been eight years since Forrest hid his treasure chest, and over 300,000 people had searched for it. Why had no one found it? I had been down this road to nowhere before. I had entered "contests" twice before that had been going on for years before I heard about them. They ended soon after I had invested a substantial amount of time, and I was not eager for an encore.

For Forrest's treasure hunt, my competition had an eight-year head start. Was someone about to solve Forrest's puzzle? If I decided to proceed, I would be at a severe disadvantage. Should I bother? I had a lot of questions and few answers.

Thus far, I had restricted my research into Forrest and his treasure hunt to the primary source material—long-form videos of interviews were best, long-form audio was next best. Short-form audio and video (those edited, so you're not sure of the context or whether the answer matches the question) and written articles, while appreciated, didn't hold much sway with me.

I needed to find out how close other searchers were to solving the puzzle. I needed a different source of information. I needed to supercharge my research. I needed to delve into the Forrest Fenn forums.

Oh my.

A quick search of the forums turned up pages of posts where searchers claimed to have already solved the puzzle or claimed they were about to solve it. Half of the searchers were already five clues deep while I had yet to get my feet wet. I was too late! I knew it!

I had three major takeaways from my stroll into the back alleyways of the searcher community. The first was deception. A few people were trying to discourage new searchers from entering the chase and throwing other searchers off-course with misinformation. My second takeaway was that the searcher community was rampant with cognitive bias. People started at the end and used a sledgehammer to pound the poem's clues into place. My third takeaway was that there existed a community-wide disagreement about almost everything. Squabbles and bickering could be seen everywhere. There was little to no collaboration. I loved it.

The low signal-to-noise ratio meant that every minute spent on the forums was a minute wasted—hoarding random noise would not help me to locate the hoard. This was all good news. The more time my competition spent on the forums, the better. I would not join the horde. Instead, I would start at the beginning and proceed with fresh eyes. I didn't look at the forums again until after Forrest had announced that someone had found the chest.

Although I don't know how he knew, Forrest insisted that his chest was still right where he had left it. The question of how close someone else might be to solving the puzzle remained, of course. Continuing would be risky.

I decided to dip my toes in a bit further by ordering Forrest's first memoir, *The Thrill of the Chase*. While waiting for the book to arrive, I continued watching videos and reading articles. I began to see patterns. One of the patterns was that many of Forrest's answers in interviews were scripted. This was expected as going off-script could cause him to slip up. Another pattern was that some of Forrest's responses were...odd. Often, the response did not fit the question. At the same time, Forrest was not shy about saying that there were some questions he would not answer. Why the peculiar answers then? There might be something there.

About a month after I got that initial email, I finished my first read-through of *The Thrill of the Chase*. One of the biggest problems I had back then was that I liked Forrest's stories so much that I would get caught up in the narrative, forget to look for hints, and then have to read the stories all over again.

My objective of proving the treasure hunt a scam had failed. I was confident that Forrest hid a treasure chest, although I still was not sold on his reasons for doing so. I was also still worried that someone else might be close to solving the poem. Not knowing where other players were on the game board was an ever-present concern.

Winter was closing in, and the end of "boots-on-the-ground" searching had arrived. Winters in the Rocky Mountains are harsh, and it would be foolish to wander through snow-packed woods in sub-zero weather looking for a treasure chest. I felt that if no one had found it by now, the chest would be safe in its hiding spot until at least the spring. Could I close the eight-year gap in the next six months? Yes, I thought. But then again, my competition had another winter to work on the puzzle as well.

And then, I was offered a job at a company doing a task I had done a thousand times before. When I chose my profession, I didn't know about Forrest's "don't do anything for more than 15 years" advice. Thirty years ago, I would have given anything for the job opportunity now before me. Thirty years later, I felt Forrest's advice in my heart even though I didn't know the words.

If I accepted the new job offer, it would boost my pay at the price of eating up all of my available time. It was a choice between the new job or trying to solve Forrest's puzzle—there wasn't time enough for both. With my wife's blessings, I moved from a frame of mind where I *had* to do something to one where I *got* to do something. I ordered Forrest's second and third memoirs and started working on a plan.

Fennology

SIT DOWN CLASS. Open up your textbooks to page 42.

As I have gone alone in there
And with my treasures bold,
I can keep my secret where,
And hint of riches new and old.

Begin it where warm waters halt
And take it in the canyon down,
Not far, but too far to walk.
Put in below the home of Brown.

From there it's no place for the meek,
The end is ever drawing nigh;
There'll be no paddle up your creek,
Just heavy loads and water high.

If you've been wise and found the blaze,
Look quickly down, your quest to cease,
But tarry scant with marvel gaze,
Just take the chest and go in peace.

So why is it that I must go,
And leave my trove for all to seek?
The answer I already know,
I've done it tired, and now I'm weak.

So hear me all and listen good,
Your effort will be worth the cold.
If you are brave and in the wood,
I give you title to the gold.

Forrest Fenn – The Thrill of the Chase

Twenty-four lines. A poem with twenty-four lines. That's what everyone had to work with. Within those twenty-four lines lie directions to a ten-inch by ten-inch section of a 200-million-acre forest. It took me a few thousand hours to read those twenty-four lines.

According to Forrest, the solution to the poem could fit on a single sticky note. Searchers, however, had painted themselves into cozy corners that they were loath to leave. Undoing preconceptions and rigid thinking will take more than one sticky note.

Before I start, it is necessary to define two words used throughout this book: "clue" and "hint." When I use the word "clue," I am talking about one of the nine clues in the poem. When I use the word "hint," I am talking about something other than the nine clues in the poem. A hint can either be inside or outside of the poem. A clue can only be inside the poem, there are only nine of them, and according to Forrest, the first clue is "Begin it where warm waters halt."

This book is divided into three major parts:

1. *GAME THEORY*. *Game Theory* discusses my approach to solving Forrest's puzzle and the method that resulted from that research. A bit of backstory about Forrest and *The Thrill of the Chase* is woven throughout this part of the book. Readers unfamiliar with the subject should start here. Readers familiar with the subject should start here as well, but I know they won't.
2. *CHAOS THEORY*. *Chaos Theory* starts at the second clue in the poem and stops just before the "blaze." It uses the clues in the poem to take you to the general location where Forrest hid the treasure, and it uses the hints in the book to keep you there. *Chaos Theory* explains much of what searchers were missing. Searchers looking to jump straight to the solution should start here. Because I know that many searchers will skip *Game Theory*, I repeat a bit of that section in *Chaos Theory* so that readers will have better context for what they are reading.
3. *CONSILIENCE*. Picking up where *Chaos Theory* leaves off, *Consilience* starts with the "blaze" and continues to the poem's last verse. This section wraps up *The Thrill of the Chase* into what, I believe most will agree, is a conclusive and satisfying ending.

Having read the synopsis above, the voices of thousands of searchers, I have no doubt, cried out in exasperation. Some may even have felt a fleeting desire to burn a few books. "Why start at the second clue? What about the first clue?"

Many searchers want answers to every question, both asked and unasked. Yet, a few searchers are still interested in the thrill of the chase. The occasional omission of a detail from the puzzle is not an oversight but a deliberate nod to those searchers, an attempt to preserve a slight sense of mystery.

Despite this, there will be skeptics. "Oh, come off it. You're just a big phony!" some of the more cynical might complain. Look at it this way: I am so utterly confident in this solution that I'm withholding the first clue. If this decision keeps you up at night, remember: Forrest once mentioned that the first clue could be reverse-engineered from the second. Since you are awake anyway, why not give it a try? Alternatively, you can await the efforts of others, who are bound to unravel the missing pieces.

In addition to the nine clues, many searchers will be interested in hearing an explanation for their favorite unsolved aberration—or hint—from Forrest's books. While I discuss many of the hints given by Forrest, I leave out more than I talk about. Forrest gave a *lot* of hints, and going over all of them would make for a boring book. That's necessary for neither the story nor the solution.

If you are a searcher who believes that understanding a specific hint was necessary to solve the puzzle, then we disagree. None of the hints were necessary. I explain my position in full within the *Game Theory* section of this book.

For those "seasoned in the soil" searchers who still have lingering questions, the methodology that led to this solution may provide the answers you seek. That methodology is explained in the *Game Theory* section of this book. Collaboration might now be the way forward. With the poem's solution unveiled, the time for contention may give way to cooperation and new discoveries.

Fair warning: this book goes into the intricate details of solving Forrest's poem and the reasoning behind the conclusion I reached. And though I tried not to make it too tedious, technical, or dry, some may think I failed at that.

If you're unfamiliar with Forrest Fenn or *The Thrill of the Chase*, consider a brief introduction through Forrest's online interviews. By listening to the man himself and forming your own opinions, you'll not only gain a more insightful reading experience but also get your treasure-hunting feet wet.

*I studied till my eyes were red
Looking for just one more thread
To find the path that I must tread
And walk where sands of time have led.*

*Although it's sound, my back feels dread
My feet like fire, my shoes like lead
To think about the chase ahead.
You're far past seventeen, I said.*

*I thought, perhaps, that I misread,
But map, and clue, and key are wed.
And so, I'll travel in your stead,
When springtime comes, and snow has fled.*

PART I
Game Theory

It's About Time

*Give me six hours to chop down a tree
and I will spend the first four sharpening the axe.*

Abraham Lincoln

FORREST FENN'S treasure hunt had been in play for eight years before I heard about it. The chase lasted ten years total, and I was starting the race at year eight. That was like running a marathon where the competition had a 20-mile head start. As far as I knew, the chest had just been stashed under the bed of some other searcher while I was reading the first page of Forrest's memoir, *The Thrill of the Chase*. I was late to the game, but I still wanted to play. The question was, could I catch up to the pack? Could I pass them?

The key to playing catch up in Forrest's game was not about years but hours. Over the previous eight years, how many hours did the other players devote to the chase in serious study? If I could match the number of hours within the next six months, I might be a contender. To do that, every spare moment I had would have to be spent working on the chase.

But it wasn't just about time, it was about quality time. A triage, of sorts, was needed to prioritize the allocation of resources, my most precious resource being time.

The first thing I did to further that goal was to exclude anything that was not a primary source or hinted at by Forrest through a primary source. I shied away from magazine and newspaper articles as well as audio and video that was lacking context. I was, however, interested in old, pre-2010, material about Forrest.

My obsession with primary source material was such that I was too diligent and excluded some sources that I shouldn't have. For instance, I didn't find out about the scrapbooks until the summer of 2019. I knew about *DalNeitzel.com*, where the scrapbooks were located, but I thought it was just another random treasure searcher's blog. I kicked myself for missing that trove of information. And, to answer the inevitable question from searchers: yes. Yes, I think there are hints in the scrapbooks—a lot of hints.

For those who don't know, the scrapbooks are short stories—mostly written by Forrest—of the same sort found in Forrest's memoirs. The scrapbooks were hosted on *DalNeitzel.com*, which is, as of this writing, no longer operational. Dal Neitzel, a friend of Forrest's, did all the dirty work needed to host Forrest's ramblings and rumblings. Forrest's third memoir, *Once Upon a While*, was created from stories in the scrapbooks, and those who paid attention to Dal's website got to read that book before it was published.

Outside of Forrest's books, if I did not personally hear Forrest make a statement, then, as far as my research was concerned, Forrest never made that statement. My distrust of written articles was so deep that, to this day, I still have not read some of them. Audio and video interviews that were lacking context were not trusted any more than written articles.

Fixating on primary source material was about giving myself the advantage of not going down someone else's rabbit hole. Time triage is not only about where to spend time, but where not to spend time, and time spent tracking down whether a supposed quote by Forrest was genuine or not was time wasted.

Within the primary source material, I still needed to prioritize where to spend the available time. For example, some of the images in *The Thrill of the Chase* seem odd, and it wouldn't surprise me if they contained a hint or two. But finding hints in images is not my forte, so I didn't travel far down that path. Similarly, I never looked at methods such as anagrams or ciphers. I thought that the poem would have already been solved if clues or major hints were encoded using those methods.

It all came down to how to best utilize the time available. I did not have the luxury of testing multiple theories. I needed to focus on the primary method I thought Forrest used to hide the clues and hints. There was, of course, a chance I could have been wrong, but I placed my bet on a deep analysis of Forrest's words.

Trying to find every advantage I could, I restricted myself to a single solution or interpretation of the poem. I would be all-in on one and only one solution. I could research multiple solutions from home, but the moment I opened the door, got in the car, and headed out to do a boots-on-the-ground search, that was it. If I was wrong, I was done.

This single solution restriction eliminated time spent on reconnaissance trips to various hunches that crossed my path. In addition to conserving time, this had the added benefit of helping to eliminate weak solutions. I had a single chip to play and was not about to place my bet unless I was well over 90% certain that there was a bronze chest waiting at the destination.

The exercise of time management and of concentrating my research into such a short timespan had enormous benefits. Everything was fresh in my mind. I could make connections between different sources of information that I would have missed had the research been spread out over several years. I am confident that 1,000 hours spent over six months, for example, was worth far more than 1,000 hours spent over six years. That I was able to start my search with access to all three of Forrest's memoirs multiplied the effect for yet another advantage.

After nine hundred hours of research, the general area where Forrest had hidden the treasure was coming into focus. One thousand hours after that, and I was standing in front of the "blaze." The effort paid off.

Shall We Play a Game?

All human errors are impatience, a premature breaking off of methodical procedure.

Franz Kafka

WITH OTHER SEARCHERS having an eight-year head start, it was necessary to spend the time I had available as wisely as possible. That concept applied not only to what source material to research but how to apply that research. It was tempting to dive right in, look at a map, and start playing hunches based on some hint I may or may not have interpreted correctly, but I knew that was a losing strategy.

Developing a methodical approach was my best chance at deciphering the clues in the poem, but that would take time. In jest, I said that it was like a marathon where the competition had a 20-mile head start, but that was not true at all. The starting line, finish line, and route were all unknown. Someone who started three months before me might have just figured out the last clue, while someone who started eight years before that might have been looking at the wrong map the entire time. There was no way to know. One thing I did know was that if someone else was so close that I did not have time for a methodical approach, then I had already lost the game.

That's what *The Thrill of the Chase* was: a winner-take-all game. There was a game designer, a referee, a playing field, a rule book, and players. A challenge was even thrown down by the game designer, "That treasure chest, I have said, is in a very special place to me. If I get another disease, on my last dying gasp, I'm going to throw myself on top of that treasure chest, and I'm going to dare you to come find me." Some form of "I dare you to go get it" was one of Forrest's often-repeated catchphrases in interviews.

My approach to Forrest's game was to reverse engineer the method Forrest had used to create the game and then develop a solution method based on the creation method. To determine how Forrest created his masterwork, I needed to look at what obstacles stood in his way. Here are a few of the significant constraints:

1. Forrest knew of the hiding spot before he decided to create the game. It was a "very special place" to him. It had to be that precise hiding spot.
2. The solution had to be solvable with just the poem and a map. Both are available for free, and anyone could play. Although other material, such as books and interviews, may provide hints, those items could not be required. Packing enough information into the poem to lead a searcher to the precise hiding spot was essential.
3. Designing such a game in the age of computers and Internet search engines would be challenging. With the sum of human knowledge available at arm's reach, any subject can be researched with ease. Difficult anagrams can be solved with a few keystrokes. Place names on maps are available with the press of a button. Custom computer programs can be written to gather, cross-reference, and analyze an unlimited amount of data. All of this had to be considered, and the game had to be resistant to it.

4. Most game designers have the luxury of play-testing their games and adjusting the difficulty based on user feedback. Because play-testing is so challenging to get right, many computer games let you set the difficulty based on your abilities and play style. Those options were not available to Forrest. Once he released his game, that was it. He either got it right, or he didn't.

The easiest way to understand all of this is to imagine yourself walking in Forrest's shoes. How would you design a game that considers every difficulty that Forrest faced? For me, answering that question was helped somewhat by knowing that Forrest's game had stood up to eight years and a few hundred thousand pairs of eyeballs.

In a sense, I was not searching for where the treasure chest was; I was searching for where the treasure chest was not. The cost of this research was time. The benefit of this research was time. I was wagering that the benefit would outweigh the cost.

"I dare you to go get it!" Challenge Accepted.

The Game Designer

Let my heart be still a moment and this mystery explore.

Edgar Allan Poe

IN MOST GAMES, knowing about the game designer does not matter. For some games, however, learning about the designer can reveal critical details about how the game was created and, possibly, how best to play it.

The stated objective of Forrest's game was to find his treasure chest. Solve the clues, find the chest, win the game. The clues led to a "very special place" to Forrest, one to which he had an "almost umbilical" connection. There was no other place that he considered hiding the chest. Forrest stressed this point so often and with such intensity that it could only mean one thing: to Forrest, the game was not about a treasure chest; it was about this special place.

This not-so-hidden subtext was all about a location that was so special to Forrest that he said he wanted to die there. Continuing and incorporating this conclusion into my methodology was troublesome for me. My initial reaction was to put the books down and step back. This was much more than a simple treasure hunt. Did I want to play this game?

After a bit of reflection, I realized that Forrest was asking for this. He wanted it. Forrest stated that his goal was to get people off their "texting machines" and out into the mountains and nature. If that was his only goal, he could have hidden the chest anywhere and kept his "very special place" secret forever, but he did not do that. He hid a chest full of gold, published a book about it, and then dared people to find it. Forrest *wanted* someone to find that special location. The treasure chest was not the objective—it was a lure, and Forrest cast that lure into a sea of people, hoping one of them would take the bait. Forrest wanted the location known to at least one person, and he was willing to pay someone to figure it out.

An alternative explanation was that the entirety of the Rocky Mountains was special to Forrest, or maybe the entirety of Yellowstone. Forrest had an "almost umbilical" connection to the Rocky Mountains as a whole and wanted to die there, "under a tree somewhere deep in a pine forest and let my body go back to the earth." This explanation does give the "getting people out into nature" statements more weight. In this day where many are glued to their computers and smartphones, the poem's creation revived an old recreation. None of that would help find the treasure chest, but it was a possibility I kept in mind.

My belief at the time was that it was the precise location that was significant. That location held a special meaning to Forrest. A similar or more scenic site a mile away wouldn't do; it had to be that exact spot. What was so special about that exact location? I had no idea, but I was certain there was more to the story than a bronze chest full of gold.

Forrest said that he intentionally inserted errors in his books to see if people would find them. Those errors were both good and bad news. While it meant that I could not trust the information in Forrest's books, it also meant the "errors" might contain hints.

Forrest hid hints amidst personal stories about his life. If searchers wanted to find the hints, they had to study and analyze Forrest's life. They had to get to know his wife, Peggy, his mother and father, his brother, Skippy, and sister, June, as well as his two wiener dogs, Bip and Tesuque. They had to read about Forrest's growing up in Temple, Texas, and traveling 1,600 miles at 35 miles per hour to Yellowstone every summer for vacation. And, if they read nothing else, according to Forrest, they should read his story, "My War For Me," included in *The Thrill of the Chase*.

The catch was, there was no way for a searcher to know whether any given statement by Forrest was accurate. Was the distance of 1,600 driving miles from Temple, Texas to Yellowstone correct? Yes, but I didn't know that. I had to measure it using the route that Forrest's family likely took back then, and that took time. If I did find an error, there was no guarantee that the error contained a hint. And even if I was sure an error contained a hint, there was no way to know whether it would be worth the time to research the error in the hopes of finding the hint.

One example of this complication is with Forrest's statement, "If Robert Redford had ever written anything he probably could have done it better than the guy who wrote that Gatsby book." That quote isn't technically an error, but it is an aberration. Robert Redford has written a book—*The Outlaw Trail: A Journey Through Time*. Was Forrest hinting at a hint? Where was the hint? Was it about outlaws? Time? Did I need to read Redford's book? Did the hint have to do with the 1974 movie, *The Great Gatsby*, starring Robert Redford? Did the fact that Ralph Lauren was the designer for the male costumes in that movie have anything to do with it? Did I need to both read The Great Gatsby and watch the film as well?

Another example is the house Forrest says he lived in as a child. According to Forrest, he grew up at 1413 Main Street, Temple, Texas. Reversing the street number gives 3141, the first four digits of "pi" (π). If Forrest had never lived at that address, then 1413/3141, as a hint, was blazing hot. If, however, Forrest did live at that address as a child, then it was only an unpolished ember. With so many of Forrest's stories involving pies, the possibility that Forrest was trying to give a hint increased. Perhaps it wasn't the number itself, but rather the act of reversing it that was key? There were several avenues to explore. Finding out whether 1413 Main Street was Forrest's childhood home would help prioritize 1413/3141 as a potential hint.

One more example: the number 328. That is the number of combat missions Forrest said he flew in Vietnam. Reading just *The Thrill of the Chase* and ignoring all other sources of information brings the number 328 into question as there is a discrepancy. On page 76, Forrest writes, "I climbed that ladder 274 times...", referring to climbing into the cockpit of his F-100 fighter jet. What about the other 54 missions? The number 328 blazes brighter when one finds out that the number of steps from Artist's Point down Lower Falls in Yellowstone is 328.

A lack of information placed the number 328 and Lower Falls high on the list of probable hints. However, further research showed that the missing 54 missions were where Forrest says he flew as a forward air controller. Even deeper research turned up a 1981 book by James Parsons titled *The Art Fever*. Within its pages, Parsons cites Forrest's 328 combat missions. The likelihood that Forrest planted a hint that far back was slim and resulted, for me, in the number 328 shifting from a high to a low probability as a potential hint. Low isn't zero, but it did help prioritize my time.

While the number 328 might not hold a hint, that still left the numbers 274 and 54. Were these numbers real or fictional? The discrepancy in *The Thrill of the Chase* made all three of the numbers stand out. The question was, did any of them hold a hint? The answer was buried in time.

Intentional insertion of "errors" was only one of the methods Forrest could have used to hide hints. Finding both the hints and the methods used to hide them would take in-depth research into Forrest's memoirs, which meant in-depth research into Forrest.

Researching the game designer was designed into the game by the designer.

The Goldilocks Zone

*Puzzles are like songs. A good puzzle can give you
all the pleasure of being duped that a mystery story can.
It has surface innocence, surprise, the revelation of
a concealed meaning, and the catharsis of solution.*

Stephen Sondheim

IT'S easy to make a game too easy. It's easy to make a game too difficult. Creating a game that's somewhere in the middle—the Goldilocks zone of not too easy and not too difficult—is another matter entirely. A game that lives in that sweet spot takes a lot of time, dedication, and resources to produce.

Although Forrest spoke often about wanting his treasure hunt to last 1,000 years, there is evidence indicating the opposite: the release of new memoirs, over 250 scrapbooks, a continuous stream of interviews, and the rain of new hints on searchers when it looked like they were not making enough progress. That does not speak of wanting the treasure hunt to last 1,000 years.

On the other hand, Forrest assuredly did not want his puzzle solved within a month or two of its release. Because of that, Forrest would have erred on the side of making his game too difficult. He could always make it easier later on.

Looking back at the release of chase-related material from Forrest, I believe he planned it something like this:

1. *Launch The Thrill of the Chase:* Publish the book and hope that the poem is not solved within the first few months.
2. *Monitor and Respond:* Read and monitor emails and online forums. Utilize various channels like scrapbooks, interviews, and websites to provide hints, all the while keeping an eye on how the hints are received.
3. *Release a Second Memoir:* If the trickle of hints isn't enough, release a second memoir with additional information.
4. *Adapt and Guide:* Assess where searchers are on the game board and strategically release more hints and memoirs to keep them moving forward. Keep adjusting the difficulty until the desired outcome is reached.

The wise thing to do would have been to plan for all of this from the beginning. Forrest did not need to finalize all of the stories, an outline or draft would suffice, leaving room for the specific details to be modified later on. This would allow him flexibility in choosing which hints to embed in which stories, as well as the timing of their release. In a general sense, the publication of this information would have been planned for. The hints were not released haphazardly—Forrest had already laid the groundwork for additional hints and the potential for more books.

The concept of easy versus difficult extended to individual hints, as well as the game as a whole. It's easy to make a hint stand out and it's easy to make a hint challenging to find. You can see this in play within *The Thrill of the Chase*, where certain stories appear well-crafted and others…not so much. When evaluating Forrest's writings outside the game, these inconsistencies become even more pronounced.

Forrest had the ability to write well, but there are aberrations in *The Thrill of the Chase* that you can't help but stumble over. They shouldn't be there. During a talk at Moby Dickens Bookstore, Forrest encouraged readers to look for "abstract things that catch up in your brain" within his book. There are quite a few of those "abstract things" in Forrest's books, and they stand out because Forrest wanted them to stand out.

That's not to say that all hints are easily discovered. My gut feeling was that the easier a hint was to find, the less valuable it likely was. With the chase having lasted eight years so far, the low-hanging fruit had, no doubt, all been picked, though not necessarily by the same person. How valuable could these easy-to-find hints be if they had not, to date, led to the end of Forrest's rainbow? There were other portions of Forrest's writings, however, which stood out in a much subtler way. I began to suspect that those passages might harbor more promising hints.

One other thing I had to take into consideration was the possibility of red herrings. Forrest could adjust the difficulty level up as well as down. Would he do that if he believed that searchers were getting too close too fast? To be thorough, I needed to account for this scenario. If Forrest did insert red herrings, I surmised that the majority would be found in the first book, *The Thrill of the Chase*. Were his references to a vast collection of works by other authors designed as mere distractions, or could there be valuable hints hidden within those volumes? Time and careful research would be required to uncover the answer.

This did not mean that Forrest's subsequent memoirs were herring-free, but the content released after *The Thrill of the Chase* did suggest a trend of Forrest's simplifying his game as it progressed. This shifting difficulty added yet another layer of complexity, underscoring the need for a methodical and analytical approach.

As a whole, that's how I would have approached the game design, and if Forrest approached it that way, then that meant that the post *Thrill of the Chase* material contained hints, and that those hints were worth the time to investigate.

In support of my theory that Forrest would have erred on the side of making his game too difficult and then making it easier as time went on, consider what happened in April 2014, almost four years after the chase began. That's the month that Forrest dropped his hint jar, and this whole mess of hints fell out:

> "Some searchers overrate the complexity of the search. Knowing about head pressures, foot pounds, acre feet, bible verses, Latin, cubic inches, icons, fonts, charts, graphs, formulas, curved lines, magnetic variation, codes, depth meters, riddles, drones or ciphers, will not assist anyone to the treasure location, although those things have been offered as positive solutions. Excellent research materials are *The Thrill of the Chase*, Google Earth, and/or a good map."
>
> Forrest Fenn — Scrapbook 62

The sudden availability of this information illustrates how Forrest's approach to the game evolved, and how he carefully controlled the level of challenge over time. For searchers considering those methods, Forrest gave them an enormous gift. That was not the act of someone who wanted the treasure chest to remain hidden for the next 1,000 years.

The Target Audience

Take nothing on its looks; take everything on evidence. There's no better rule.

Charles Dickens

FOR TYPICAL GAMES, the target audience needs to be defined and considered. *The Thrill of the Chase* was not a typical game. Far more important than the target audience was the likely audience. If Forrest filled a bronze chest with a million dollars in gold and hid it somewhere in the Rocky Mountains, who might want to play that game? Everyone? Could knowledge of the audience (both target and likely) for *The Thrill of the Chase* help solve Forrest's game? I believed so.

For typical games, it does not matter whether those outside the target audience play the game. The designer of a typical game does not have to make the game resistant to players with attributes that differ from the target audience. If others play the game, who cares? *The Thrill of the Chase*, however, was a one-shot, winner-take-all game. If Forrest had a preferred audience, could he make the game solvable for that audience while at the same time making it resistant to those outside of that audience? That would depend quite a bit on the target audience.

For typical games, game designers need to ask themselves what combination of attributes the expected player base will have. Examples include age, education, intelligence, background, knowledge, perspective, nationality, culture, and language. When Forrest asked himself about the attributes of his potential player base, the answers were, undoubtedly, "Yes." Even if Forrest had a preferred group in mind when designing his game, he had to expect that everyone was a potential player.

How do you make a game that resists three hundred thousand people from all backgrounds and abilities trying to solve it for eight years in the age of the Internet? A game that one person finds straightforward, another person may find a mind-bending pretzel of confusion. More important than that, what may have seemed challenging to Forrest may have been elementary for some unknown searcher. But Forrest did that. Forrest made that game. That Forrest did so was, I believe, an actionable hint.

How do you make a game that resists three hundred thousand people from all backgrounds and abilities trying to solve it for eight years in the age of the Internet? You start by anticipating what tools people will have at their disposal and design the game to resist those tools. In this case, the two tools that stood out most were computers and the Internet.

Difficult anagrams, for example, can now be solved using a computer. Consequently, I relegated anagrams to a lower position on my list of probable clue-hiding methods. While Forrest may have released a hint or two using anagrams, I did not believe the poem was encoded in this way. This rationale extended to any method where a computer could shoulder the majority of the analytical work. While I could have been wrong and taking that approach carried a certain level of risk, I calculated the risk to be low. It was a conscious and deliberate decision, based on my understanding of Forrest's methodology and the tools and time available to us both.

As another example, part of the likely audience for Forrest's treasure hunt was sure to be searchers experienced with other treasure hunts. It seemed inevitable that these individuals would approach solving Forrest's puzzle using similar strategies that had been successful in other hunts. Yet, given that after eight years no one had cracked Forrest's mystery, it strongly implied that he had not employed those methods. Thus, like anagrams, those techniques were relegated to a lower position on my list of probable clue-hiding methods.

The examples above concern the likely audience for Forrest's treasure hunt, exploring how Forrest might have anticipated the techniques they would employ to decode his puzzle, and how he could thwart those strategies. But what about the target audience? Did Forrest have a specific or preferred audience in mind for his treasure hunt, or was the target audience the same as the likely audience? Forrest provided an answer to this question, but since it's Forrest—interpreting the answer is a puzzle of its own. In true Forrest fashion, the answer may not lie in the words themselves but rather in the nuanced spaces between them.

There were certain remarks that Forrest made in nearly every interview, and one of those remarks was some variation about his target audience: "My audience is every redneck in Texas with a pickup truck, a wife, twelve kids, and he lost his job," Forrest would say while laughing. What did Forrest mean with this "redneck" statement, and why did he keep repeating it?

The first possibility was that the remark should be taken at face value—rednecks were Forrest's target audience. If so, he might have been hinting that the chest was somewhere near where an unemployed redneck from Texas with a wife and twelve kids could afford to visit. New Mexico is a lot closer to Texas than Montana.

Another possibility was that the remark was just a funny line to give an interviewer something to quote. From his days running Fenn Galleries, Forrest knew all about marketing, how to handle the press, and how to get the most mileage from an interview. A line like that could push Forrest's story to the front page.

Yet another possibility was that the remark was a hint-delivery mechanism. To find out if the statement contained a hint, I would need to dissect it. That would take time, and as I've said, my success or failure depended on how I managed time.

Of all the possibilities, I felt that the marketing angle was the most probable. That did not mean that the other possibilities were wrong; they were not mutually exclusive.

Assigning a "most probable" status to the marketing tactic was a strategic decision to help me prioritize my time and focus. If other avenues of investigation didn't pan out, I might swing back around and look for hints in the redneck statement. With that in mind, I simply added the analysis of this statement to my task list under the heading "Things to do to find Forrest's treasure," and then set it aside. I didn't need to pick it back up. The research into the likely audience was enough.

The Playing Field

Short cuts make long delays.

J. R. R. Tolkien

"IN THE MOUNTAINS somewhere north of Santa Fe." Those were Forrest's first words describing where he hid the treasure. Many took Forrest's statement to mean that the treasure was hidden in New Mexico even though Forrest clarified the message early on. In August 2011, less than one year after *The Thrill of the Chase* was published, reporter Gadi Schwartz recounts an interview with Forrest, "Just because he said it's in the mountains north of Santa Fe doesn't mean it's in New Mexico. The mountains in Alaska are north of Santa Fe." The Swiss Alps are also north of Santa Fe.

What's the implication here—did that mean the entire northern hemisphere was fair game? That's a big playing field. Thankfully, Forrest clarified his statement further when he started using the phrase, "in the Rocky Mountains north of Santa Fe." Depending on how you interpreted Forrest's original remark, that either narrowed or widened the playing field.

In 2013, Forrest released his second memoir, *Too Far To Walk*, which contained a map of the search area. And although the Rockies go up into Canada, Forrest's map stopped at the Canadian border. That left Montana, Wyoming, Colorado, and New Mexico. The map also ruled out private lands with the assertion, "Forrest Fenn's hidden treasure is somewhere to be found within the highlighted region of the Rocky Mountains on this map." The only highlighted regions on that map are public lands and, if you zoom in and compare Forrest's map with a land ownership map, you will see that the non-highlighted regions match well with private lands.

One thing to note about the *Too Far to Walk* map is that it is an artistic map first and foremost. While the map is mostly accurate, someone painted its colors with a broad brush. Out on the edges, where the highlighted colors meet, searchers cannot rely on the accuracy of that map. I can say with certainty that some lands shown on that map as one type of public land are, in fact, a different type of public land. The same goes for public lands shown as private and private lands shown as public, not to mention several land designations that the map ignores entirely.

When Forrest said that all you needed was the poem and a good map, he was *not* talking about the *Too Far to Walk* map. While it is a nice-looking map, it was not the best map for *The Thrill of the Chase* treasure hunters.

Why, then, is the map riddled with errors? In my opinion, the errors are a simple byproduct of trying to make it aesthetically pleasing. The errors do not compromise the map's three primary functions: to define the Rocky Mountains, to identify where the treasure was located, and to identify where the treasure was not located.

As shown in the map's legend, five land designations are highlighted, each represented by its own unique color. These lands are Bureau of Land Management lands, National Forest lands, National Parks, Fish and Wildlife Service lands, and Tribal lands.

Where was the treasure located? On land in the highlighted part of the map. Where was it not located? On land in the unhighlighted part of the map. This was a more significant hint than it may at first appear, but it also brought up a complication. That the map is inaccurate regarding land ownership is both provable and problematic.

If Forrest had said the treasure was on Bureau of Land Management land, for instance, the map could mislead. Do I go by the highlighted color of a particular portion of the map, even if I am confident that the section shown should not be highlighted in that color, or should the map and the legend be treated separately?

My eventual decision was to treat the map and the legend separately. A map legend is, by definition, a key. It gives instruction on how to read a map. This legend provided five possible land ownership designations indicating where Forrest could have hidden the treasure chest. It eliminated everything else, including private lands, state forests, school trust lands, city-owned lands, and military bases. The map's legend mentioned none of those, and so I dropped all of those from consideration.

Some searchers may point out that Forrest refused to rule out private land, saying he didn't want to narrow the search area. Allow me to interpret and rephrase that statement. In my opinion, Forrest did not want to narrow the search area by spoon-feeding people the correct interpretation of the hints he gave. With the release of the *Too Far to Walk* map and the statement about the treasure being in the highlighted area of that map, Forrest *did* narrow the search area. Forrest released a map that narrowed the search area, told everyone how to read it, and then left it up to the individual to do so.

Over the years, Forrest narrowed the search area even further with a series of undeniably clear declarations, such as:

- The treasure was not in Idaho, Nevada, or Utah.
- The treasure was located above 5,000 feet and below 10,200 feet.
- The treasure was not in a mine, a tunnel, a graveyard, an outhouse, or under water.
- The treasure was not near the Rio Grande river.

I wasn't complaining. I don't think I would have ever limited myself to New Mexico, but I would have considered private lands.

*

The "playing field," as described above, was likely what most searchers had in mind as they looked for the treasure. However, this viewpoint is fundamentally flawed. That was not the playing field at all. *Everything above refers to the treasure's location and only the treasure's location.*

Technically speaking, the playing field encompassed the entire world. Clues could begin in the Rocky Mountains, venture beyond them, only to return later. Or the clues might echo Forrest's annual migratory treks as a child, starting in Temple Texas, and threading through states like New Mexico, Colorado, and Wyoming, before finally arriving in West Yellowstone, Montana. The clues might even trace Forrest's global travels, from the U.S., to Germany, to Tripoli, to Vietnam, and then back to the U.S. As long as the clues concluded in the highlighted portion of the *Too Far to Walk* map, all paths were open.

Naturally, some scenarios were more plausible than others, necessitating a prioritization based on the likelihood of each possibility. The number of *potential* paths, however, extends far beyond what is initially apparent, demonstrating the complexity and intrigue of Forrest's treasure hunt.

The Rulebooks

All games are meaningless if you do not know the rules.

B. K. S. Iyengar

THE GOOD NEWS was that Forrest's rulebook for playing the game was simple and easy to follow: "If you can find it, you can have it." That was it. That was the entirety of Forrest's rulebook for how to play his game and, while it wasn't helpful, it was concise.

It was easy to start playing Forrest's game. The only problem was that you had no way of knowing how well or poorly you were playing. The lack of a feedback loop was, of course, by design. In a way, it was comical. It was like a multi-state scavenger hunt with 300,000 players, each picking their own starting line, route, and finish line, and each running off in different directions as fast as they could go. And I was about to be player number 300,001.

More helpful, but less concise and harder to unravel, was Forrest's rulebook for how he created the game. Being able to identify *that* rulebook was one of the benefits of starting the game eight years late.

Forrest often talked about his "list of rules," usually giving an example or two. Gathering together and looking at Forrest's "creation rules" all at once makes them stand out much more so than looking at them scattered across time. Here are some of the rules Forrest used to create his game:

> *"To me, rules were a guide."*
> *"You know, I've never wanted to break a serious rule, but I stretched the hell out of a few."*
> *"I broke all the rules of custom."*
> *"Why do I have to live by everybody else's rules?"*
> *"What's wrong with making your own rules about things?"*
> *"I made up a lot of rules to protect myself."*
> When asked whether he had followed the rules of capitalization throughout the entire poem, Forrest replied, *"Whose rules?"*
> *"Who made the rule that says I shouldn't end a sentence with a preposition?"*
> *"I am frequently criticized for where I put commas. My reply is that I don't want to use anybody's book-writing rules."*
> *"I don't have any rules."*
> *"I was going to make it work no matter what."*

Some may think that these are not rules at all but rather Forrest's thoughts on rules. That is incorrect. The list above is a perfect encapsulation of Forrest's rulebook for creating his treasure hunt. "I don't have any rules" was a rule in and of itself. In regards to Forrest's creation of his game, there were no rules; there was only the objective of "I was going to make it work no matter what."

Finding Forrest's thoughts about rules was fantastic news. It fit right into the methodology that was forming in my mind on how to approach the solution. It also helped firm up the suspicion I had that Forrest's treasure hunt was about much more than a box of gold. "I was going to make it work no matter what" for a simple treasure hunt—a hunt that had to end at a pre-determined location to which Forrest had an "almost umbilical" attachment? No, this was not an ordinary treasure hunt.

Forrest provided a rulebook for how he created the game and a rulebook for playing the game. Now I needed a rulebook for how to solve the game, and I had just stumbled over the answer: There were no rules, there were only possibilities and probabilities, and that was a game I knew how to play.

Possibilities and Probabilities

Probable impossibilities are to be preferred to improbable possibilities.

Aristotle

I NEED to clarify my statements regarding "no rules." When I talked about Forrest's creation rules, I meant that Forrest would not abide by anyone else's rules, not that he did not have rules of his own. While Forrest may have started with the objective of "I was going to make it work no matter what," the rules he created along the way were what allowed him to achieve that objective. I aimed to find that set of rules.

For my attempt at solving Forrest's puzzle, "no rules" meant that, because I did not know what Forrest's rules were, everything was in play simultaneously. Everything was a hint, and nothing was a hint. Everything was a red herring, and nothing was a red herring. Every statement uttered by Forrest held a possible hint or herring or maybe both. I loved it. It was as if Forrest was encouraging me to play where I was most comfortable.

This was all more of a self-evident observation than a reasoned conclusion. If it was impossible to know whether any given fragment of information contained a hint, then the "hint-state" of each fragment was unknown. That is, for each fragment of information, there was a possibility that it contained a hint and a possibility that it did not contain a hint. Stating this may seem obvious, but being disciplined about the thought process throughout the search was crucial.

"Everything was in play at the same time" meant not just the words in the books and the interviews, but...everything:

- The design, history, and age of the bronze chest.
- The $25,000 Forrest said he paid for the chest.
- The chest contents, including the number of coins in the chest, the types of coins, the frogs, the dragon bracelet, the turquoise row bracelet, the emerald ring, and the necklace with thirty-nine animal fetishes.

"Everything" also meant everything seemingly unrelated to the treasure hunt, including:

- Forrest's pets.
- The eight bells and jars Forrest said he had buried.
- Forrest's other published books.
- The purple sweater he always wore.
- The names he gave to his shoes.
- Everything surrounding his military career.
- Anything else tangentially related to Mr. Forrest Fenn.

These pieces of information were in play simultaneously in a 3D matrix of connected and fluctuating possibilities and probabilities. Individual clues and hints could influence one another. If a new hint popped into existence or an old hint popped out, everything else would need to adjust to the presence or absence of that hint.

One way to visualize this is to view clues and hints as celestial objects in a solar system interconnected by a gravitational force. Each object exerts influence on the others, determined by its position and mass. If you move or remove an object, the entire system must adjust. The larger the object, the more significant its influence on surrounding objects.

A simplified view of this model would view the clues as planets, with the hints as moons orbiting the planets. Add in a few hints that are so large they earn dwarf-planet status and have hints of their own. Throw in several rogue, comet-sized hints that roam the system. Then, tie it all together with an asteroid field of red herrings.

Other than the nine clues, I had no idea what belonged in this imaginary solar system. I knew neither where the objects were located in relation to one another nor their importance. One thing I suspected, though, was that the system would not be random, and it would not be chaotic. It would be harmonious. Another thing I suspected was that to be complete, the system needed something in the center around which everything revolved. That thing was not a clue, and it was not a hint; it was the purpose of the game.

The clues in the poem were easier to deal with than the hints. There were only nine clues within the 24 verses of the poem, while there were an unknown number of hints scattered throughout everything else Forrest had ever written or said. Although, if I were to apply my "everything was possible" mantra thoroughly, even the nine clues were in question. I gave that a low probability.

One layer of significant difficulty that needed to be factored in was that each possible clue and hint had its own list of possible interpretations. There were possibilities within possibilities, each with its own probability.

Another layer of difficulty was that the clues and hints could not be solved in isolation. A clue might have a half-dozen equally strong interpretations, but at most, only one of those could be correct. Choosing one interpretation for a clue in isolation from the other clues would be nothing more than guesswork.

That clues and hints could not be solved in isolation was an integral part of my methodology. Each interpretation of a clue or hint would only connect to specific interpretations of surrounding clues and hints. If I were to create an exhaustive list of interpretations for clues and hints and then try to connect the dots, what would come out the other side?

Those familiar with Forrest's memoirs and material related to the chase may be shaking their heads at all this. Forrest wrote a *lot* of stories about a *lot* of subjects, all with colorful language and intentional aberrations that would hook the unwary reader. If everything was possible, then there were too many possibilities, and my method would try to solve for every one of them. That is correct, and that was the point. But all solutions are not created equal, and I was only interested in one of them.

To navigate through that ocean of possibilities, I needed some way to rank solutions relative to one another to find the only solution that mattered.

The Referee

What are the facts? Again and again and again—what are the facts? Shun wishful thinking, ignore divine revelation, forget what "the stars foretell," avoid opinion, care not what the neighbors think, never mind the unguessable "verdict of history"—what are the facts, and to how many decimal places? You pilot always into an unknown future; facts are your single clue. Get the facts!

Robert Heinlein

IT HAD BEEN eight years since Forrest's game began, and searchers were still widely divided on where Forrest hid the treasure chest. Searchers were hiking through the woods in all four of the search states, and, presumably, most of those searchers were confident about where they were looking. Why were they all so confident when most of them were not even in the correct state? I thought I knew why, and I thought I had a solution for that problem.

I needed an objective referee to look at my work, and tell me how well I was doing. I couldn't be my own referee, and Forrest didn't accept the job offer, so I designed an impartial construct to be the ultimate arbiter of my ideas. I came up with a 100-point scoring system with which to evaluate potential solutions. I built the system around the following suppositions:

1. There were nine clues in the 24 verses of the poem.
2. Every word was important, especially the nouns. "Each word is deliberate," Forrest had said.
3. The poem could be solved without the book.
4. The poem was "straightforward with no subterfuge in sight."

I named the resulting system the "Finite Operational Rules to Rate the Estimated Strength of a Theory."

I assigned an "Interpretation Score" to each clue, each verse, and how well everything flowed from one verse to the next. The highest possible cumulative score was 99.5, meaning that, without the treasure chest in hand, I could only be a maximum of 99.5% sure of a solution's accuracy. Holding the chest itself was worth the last 0.5%. A simplified view of the scoring system is shown below:

- 7 points maximum for the interpretation of each clue. 63 points total.
- 1 point maximum for the interpretation of each verse of the poem. 24 points total. This addressed verses that contain important words but not a clue and was independent of whether the verse also contained a clue.
- 0.5 points maximum for the connection between each verse and its successor. 11.5 points total. How well does one verse flow into the next? While I felt that the connections were important, there was a possibility that not all verses had satisfying connections to surrounding verses. Because of this, I didn't want to give the connections too much weight.
- 1 point if the solution explained the meaning of the game. Explanations such as "Because the area was pretty" or "It was his favorite fishing hole" earned zero

points. I was sure there was a deeper meaning to Forrest's game. Although it was only one point, finding a persuasive meaning might be the deciding factor on whether I committed to a solution.
- 0.5 points if I were holding the chest at the identified location.

For each verse and each potential clue, I created a list of plausible interpretations. I then rated each interpretation on a 1 to 10 point scale based on how well I thought the interpretation fit the poem. This was a "strength modifier." Although these ratings were subjective, I did make a conscious effort to suppress my biases. What was more important was that generating and rating the interpretations occur before I tried to match the poem to a map.

At this point of the analysis, I neither knew nor cared which poem verses contained the nine clues—I was just looking for different interpretations of everything written. I also didn't care about the strength of an interpretation. I wasn't looking for strong interpretations, I was looking for all possible interpretations. I got excited with each new idea, even if I felt it was incorrect. Even after "solving" a particular verse of the poem, I was still on the lookout for and would document new interpretations for that verse should any ever present themselves.

The Interpretation Scores for each verse and each potential clue were modified using the formula: [Maximum Points * Strength Modifier * 0.1]. For example, an interpretation for a clue (7 points maximum) with a strength modifier of 10 would get the full 7 points. An interpretation for a clue with a strength modifier of 5, on the other hand, would end up with 3.5 points.

Individual interpretations for each part of the poem could be combined in various sequences to form different sets of interpretations for the poem as a whole. Each of these sets would stand as a potential solution to the poem. After all Interpretation Scores were adjusted by all modifiers, the individual Interpretation Scores could be added together to produce a "Cumulative Interpretation Score" for each set. If everything went according to plan, the correct solution would be exposed. It would have the highest Cumulative Interpretation Score.

There was a risk here. What if I gave Forrest's actual interpretation of a clue a low strength-modifier? It was a near guarantee that our opinions would differ, at least a little, here and there. While this meant that I was unlikely to find a solution with a 99.5 Cumulative Interpretation Score, our opinions shouldn't be so far apart that I would dismiss the correct solution out of hand. At least I hoped they wouldn't. If our thinking was so out of sync that my scoring system returned less than 90 for the correct solution, then all this would be nothing more than a fun, but failed, mental exercise as I would not have walked out the front door to test a solution with such a low score.

"What about the hints?" some may ask. "Shouldn't they be factored into the scoring system?" I believed that the hints were what was throwing everybody off. Throw a dart at a map, and I'll find a hint that fits wherever the dart landed, even if the dart missed the map. Questionable hints found while in the field didn't help. Combine all that with cognitive bias, and the result is what was happening in the chase: searchers divided between Colorado, Montana, New Mexico, and Wyoming. Hints were thus relegated to confirmation duty only and played no part in the scoring of potential solutions.

What about Forrest's implying that there was a boots-on-the-ground component to the chase? That's true; Forrest did imply that. The most probable meaning was the blaze: "If you've been wise and found the blaze..." Forrest confirmed that the blaze was a single physical object, and it was possible that finding it would require a physical presence. But there was a high probability that the blaze was a clue, not a hint. *All* of the clues could require a physical presence as far as I was concerned—as long as they fit the poem, matched to locations on a map, and received strong Interpretation Scores. Hints, however, could only serve as confirmers or as pointers to clues.

Forrest's assertion that searchers could solve the poem without the books was one of the main arguments for handling hints this way. If I could ignore the books in their entirety, I could ignore all of the hints in the books. No matter how loudly some passage was screaming, *"LOOK AT ME, I'M A HINT!"* an understanding of that hint's meaning was not necessary for the solution. That thinking was baked into my methodology.

The biggest problem with basing a solution around hints is that you must then discount all conflicting hints, and no matter the hint, there are always conflicting hints. My methodology dealt with that problem handily.

Although it may sound like I am minimizing the hints, especially hints external to the poem, that is not the case. I am just emphasizing that hints are nowhere near as important as the clues in the poem. The poem and a map, by themselves, can lead to the treasure's location. The hints, a map, and anything else you can think of —*without the poem*—cannot do that.

What role, then, do the hints play? In Part Two of this book —*Chaos Theory*—I describe how the first four clues brought me to the general vicinity where Forrest hid the treasure and how confirmations from the hints kept me there, searching for more clues. Although the interpretations of those initial clues each earned a high Interpretation Score, they seemed almost deceptively simple. Presented with just the clues and without the accompanying hints, many would dismiss this portion of the solution as too easy. Yet, upon grasping the hints, those same people would be planning a trip for the next day.

As far as judging a solution, the only thing that mattered was the poem. All the hints in the world would not increase the Cumulative Interpretation Score of a solution by a single point. This restriction meant that the poem had to be solved. Nine clues, each with a strong individual Interpretation Score, had to be identified. Each verse in the poem had to have an equally strong Interpretation Score. And they all had to flow together into a perfect union of ideas pointing to a ten-inch by ten-inch section of the Rocky Mountains.

Constant as the Northern Star

There are no facts, only interpretations.
Friedrich Nietzsche

THERE IS another category of information provided by Forrest that exists somewhere between a hint and a clue: Constants. Constants were statements of fact, such as:

- There are nine clues in the poem.
- Searchers can solve the poem without the book.
- The clues are consecutive, contiguous, and chronological.
- The treasure is located above 5,000 feet and below 10,200 feet.
- The treasure is not in a mine, a tunnel, a graveyard, an outhouse, or under water.
- "There isn't a human trail in very close proximity" to where Forrest hid the treasure chest.
- "Begin it where warm waters halt" is the first clue.

I designed my methodology around the idea of there being no such thing as constants, only possibilities and probabilities. How best, then, to address constants? If genuine, they could be immensely helpful. But if even one purported constant was not what it seemed, I might never find the correct solution.

The idea of treating constants as irrefutable facts made my gut tighten in distaste; "Things are never what they seem with Forrest" was fast becoming my number one rule. To reconcile this, I chose to assess constants using the same interpretation points concept that I applied to the clues and hints. I would treat constants like any other element: breaking them down into possible interpretations and assigning each an Interpretation Score.

That was my official position on the matter, and it satisfied my gut. In practice, though, I took what seemed to me the most obvious interpretation of each constant, assigned it a 99.9% probability of being correct, and did not dwell on other interpretations. However, 99.9 is not 100 (at least in my universe), so constants were subject to future scrutiny should the situation warrant it. That satisfied my desire not to get bogged down in too many details.

I considered creating an Interpretation Score modifier based on constants but doubted it was worth the time. Instead, I created a straightforward checklist composed of statements made by Forrest that might serve as confirmations for a solution. Every potential solution was subject to having to answer the questions in the checklist. While I had no specific "passing grade" in mind, anything less than a full 100% would have given me a bit of anxiety.

Here are some of the confirmers, based on constants, that made it onto the checklist:

- Did this solution come from just the poem and a map?
- Is Forrest's "if Yellowstone erupts, the treasure will not be blown to bits" statement explained?
- Is Forrest's "walk with confidence" statement explained?
- Is Forrest's "kids may have an advantage" remark explained?

- Is the "very special place" special for a very special reason?

I gave my list of constants a higher status than hints. Hints are hidden, constants are out in the open. Hints have to be interpreted, constants do not. Searchers largely disagree on the hints, and largely agree on constants. Constants should be true no matter the solution, while the interpretation of hints may change depending on the solution. I didn't feel the need to explain any specific hint or aberration, but I did feel the need to explain the items on the list of constants.

There was one statement of fact that I was hoping was not a constant: a proxy item for the treasure chest. Forrest insisted that the back-breaking 42 combined pounds of the chest and contents were really out there and that there was no proxy item with a phone number that you call to get the key to a vault somewhere. You had to carry the chest out physically. Test hikes with a 25-pound bag of rice in my backpack settled it. My back convinced the rest of me to remove the "there is no proxy item" qualification from the checklist —I would have been delighted to have a proxy lighten my load.

All this was subjective, I admit. Nevertheless, I wasn't trying to convince anyone else; I was trying to convince myself. I restricted myself to a single solution to the poem and there was a high price to pay for letting cognitive bias take over. If my solution was incorrect and I were to make a boots-on-the-ground trip to wherever that incorrect solution directed me, it would invoke my one-solution-only rule, and I would have wasted my only chance.

Because of that, I was my own toughest critic, testing my solutions and trying to find flaws. One particular test illustrates this point well: *Would most searchers be so convinced of this solution that if I renounced it, they would not believe me?* Casting aside a weak or mediocre solution to the poem would be met with a predictable "obviously that's not it." But the real solution—Forrest's solution—should be of such high quality and resonate so deeply that most every searcher, unless blinded by their preconceptions, would recognize and acknowledge its authenticity. *That* was the solution I was looking for.

Lost in Translation

*The single biggest problem in communication
is the illusion that it has taken place.*

George Bernard Shaw

SEVERAL THINGS STOOD out in Forrest's interviews, but the part I found most interesting was his continued emphasis on the meanings of words. Forrest said he looked up every word in the poem, to be sure of what it meant. He said that each word was deliberate, and it was risky to discount any of them. And for some reason, he had an odd need to make people aware of his favorite definition of the word "several."

Forrest made sure that specific topics, like the meanings of words, were covered in every interview. If an interview was not going in a direction that would bring these topics up naturally, Forrest would interject them unnaturally. Was Forrest trying to tell people how to play the game? Did anyone listen?

Forrest said it was possible to walk with confidence to the treasure chest using just the 166 words in the poem and a map. And yet, after eight years, the chest was still in hiding. What method could

Forrest have used to lead to this outcome? I had several ideas on how I thought Forrest disguised the clues, and the first idea that came to mind had to do with the meanings of words.

I have always had a passing interest in linguistics and especially with semantics. Semantics is the branch of linguistics and logic concerned with meaning, not only of words but with all aspects of communication. For instance, one thing I've noticed is that no matter how well constructed a sentence, with a large enough audience, there's invariably at least one person who will misinterpret the intended meaning. As I write this book, I cannot help but speculate how my thoughts may be misconstrued.

I've long maintained that no two people on earth truly speak the same language. Every word carries multiple shades of meaning. When I communicate, I rely on my "internal translator" to convert my thoughts into words based on my unique understanding of those words. Others process these words through their internal translators, applying their understanding to those same words. This is where communication starts to break down.

Consider the word "several," for example. If my preferred definition of the word "several," does not match your preferred definition of that word, then what I've said is not what you've heard. We might continue our conversation, each believing we have grasped the other's meaning, but in reality, we haven't. The longer the conversation persists, the more opportunities arise for misunderstanding.

Most of the time, these miscommunications are subtle. The comedian Brian Regan gives a not-so-subtle example about the meaning of the word "pie." Growing up in Florida, Brian had thought that pie meant...pie. Having grown up in New Jersey, Brian's roommate in college had a different definition for that word. The roommate was going to order a pie; what kind of pie did Brian want? They got half pepperoni and half pumpkin.

These breakdowns in communication are commonplace and can be seen in any conversation that lasts more than a few moments. If you are looking for examples, look no further than people discussing what Forrest said on any given topic. And if you see words in quotes attributed to Forrest, best ask for and double-check the source.

Most who misquote Forrest do so sincerely, not intending to deceive. Searchers translated Forrest's words into a personal meaning, which were translated back again using different words and unintentional distortions. Forrest's meaning was lost in translation.

This simple, yet profound, reality underscores the complexities of language and interpretation. It serves as a reminder that even the most seemingly straightforward statements can be subject to varying interpretations. I believed that Forrest may have used these linguistic nuances as tools to keep his secret safe.

Communication goes beyond the definition of individual words. Tone and inflection provide emphasis and emotion. The same sentence using the same words in the same order can have different meanings based on which word is emphasized. Edward Sapir, in his paper, "The Status of Linguistics as a Science," wrote:

> "The understanding of a simple poem, for instance, involves not merely an understanding of the single words in their average significance, but a full comprehension of the whole life of the community as it is mirrored in the words, or as it is suggested by their overtones."
>
> Edward Sapir

The Thrill of the Chase was not simply about communication. It was about a game, where communication was key. In Forrest's game, nothing could be discounted, and that includes pronunciation. Veteran searchers will be familiar with Forrest's story about the Popo Agie River near Lander, Wyoming. Some of those searchers are quick to point out that Forrest's pronunciation of Popo Agie was incorrect, but was it?

Forrest pronounced "Agie" the same as "Aggie," as in the stouthearted "Aggies" of Texas A&M University that Forrest wrote about. Aggie—as in the marbles that Forrest made in Miss Ford's Spanish class instead of studying. Forrest made those marbles from agate rocks found in Yellowstone—agate rocks which were also used to create line guides for fishing poles, like the guide for the tip of Forrest's fly rod. Agate—as in an agate font, used in typography and noted as the smallest point size that can be printed and remain legible—necessary for Forrest's goal of including his autobiography in the treasure chest by placing it in a small olive jar sealed with wax.

Communication, under ideal circumstances, can be challenging. In *The Thrill of the Chase*, Forrest was playing a game of trying to communicate hints to searchers without being too obvious about it. Was Forrest trying to share something with his pronunciation of "Popo Agie?" Just as each word in the poem was deliberate and it was risky to discount any of those words, I suspected that Forrest's mispronunciations were intentional, and correcting any of them was just as risky.

People have long utilized the art of wordplay and the subtle manipulation of language to create secret codes and messages understood only by select individuals. If I were tasked with devising a hunt similar to Forrest's, I would undoubtedly consider employing such a method. Could Forrest's famous quote, "It's not who you are, it's who they think you are," be rephrased as, "It's not what you say, it's what they think you say?"

Forrest's third memoir, *Once Upon a While*, provided a possible confirmation of this line of thought. At the end of most chapters in that book is a stylized post-office cancellation mark with the phrase, "My Two Sense." Did substituting "sense" for "cents" hold a hint? One definition of "sense" is "The meaning of a word or phrase in a specific context, especially as isolated in a dictionary or glossary; the semantic element in a word or group of words." Did that speak of doublespeak—"My Two Meanings?"

The likelihood that Forrest used the meanings of words to conceal the clues and hints seemed increasingly probable to me. But time was limited. Dissecting each word of the poem (and many words within the books) and then reconstructing them with alternative meanings felt like deciphering a cryptic language known to no one else—and was a task that demanded an immense investment of time. Should I invest that time? This was a pivotal decision. Choose wisely, and I was still in the game. Choose poorly, and time would fly by while I was stuck in reverse.

Eight years. I kept coming back to 300,000 people playing this game over the previous eight years. Surely other searchers had considered alternate meanings of words as a method Forrest might have used to hide clues and hints. If Forrest did use that method, why hadn't the treasure been discovered by now?

I kept coming to the same conclusion: If Forrest had used any single method to hide the clues, the game would already be over. That was the answer. Forrest did not rely on just one method. Instead, he crafted a polymorphic puzzle, employing multiple techniques to conceal the clues. This multi-layered complexity could explain the eight-year search without a solution, despite the efforts of hundreds of thousands of searchers from around the world. It also aligns with Forrest's assertion that "the treasure may be located by the one who can best adjust," which might have been intended as a warning against rigid thinking and adherence to a singular approach.

That realization marked a turning point. I was on the brink of overanalyzing and recognized the need to commit to a path. Not only did I believe that "Fennglish"—my coined term for Forrest's coded language—was one of the methods Forrest used to hide clues and hints, but I felt a growing conviction about the polymorphic nature of the poem as well. It is with those two concepts that I staked my claim. I hoped that I had chosen wisely.

Through the Looking Glass

The most difficult thing is the decision to act, the rest is merely tenacity.

Amelia Earhart

THE GAMBIT WAS SET, and, like Alice, I stood on the brink of the unexpected. The world felt different on this side of the decision, and I was about to discover if the chosen approach would lead to clarity or complexity. There were indications that Forrest used at least three methods to conceal the clues. In the early stages of the treasure hunt, Forrest revealed that some had deciphered the first two clues, stating, "Searchers continue to figure the first two clues." Sometime later, Forrest said, "Some may have solved the first four clues, but I am not certain." Apparently, one could guess at the first two clues, while the second two were considerably more challenging. Beyond the fourth clue, Forrest remained tight-lipped, only warning that starting with the "blaze" was unlikely to bring success.

This led me to suspect that the first two clues were encoded using the same method, if they were encoded at all. Then, there was a switch in the method for the next two clues and perhaps another shift at the fifth clue. I had no idea how far into the poem searchers had reached, but at the time, I thought it likely that this pattern of switching methods persisted throughout.

The idea that the poem was polymorphic, changing and adapting in form, gained traction in my mind. It seemed highly probable, considering the evidence, and it became a central theme in my research. A poem that morphed midstream could easily throw searchers off the trail. Without clear confirmations within the poem itself, many might abandon a winning solution upon hitting a perceived roadblock. This ingenious design seemed to be working exactly as intended, keeping the treasure hidden and the searchers guessing.

Forrest's numerous comments about searchers finding the first two clues proved to be a huge hint. I suggested above that there were no known mid-poem confirmations. While that was true at the beginning of the chase, the situation had evolved by the time I joined. Forrest had generously provided those validations.

The first confirmation was that many searchers had "solved" and were continuing to solve the first two clues in the poem. This suggested that the first two clues were obvious. This "obviousness" affected how I judged my solution. If my interpretations for the first two clues were not obvious, they were not correct.

The second confirmation was that all or nearly all of the people who solved the first two clues did not make it to the third. This indicated that there must be a substantial complication with either the third clue itself or in the path from the second to the third, and my solution needed to identify the obstacle. Discovering a potential interpretation of the third clue that offered a convincing solution for this riddle gave me an enormous boost in confidence.

Working on the premise that there were different clue-encoding methods necessitated identifying methods by which the clues might be encoded. Some of the methods I was on the lookout for were:

- Information that one could only obtain in the field. This was bolstered by Forrest's remarks that he did not think anyone could solve the entire poem from home.

- Pareidolia in situ. I hoped this was not the case because I am terrible at identifying images from random patterns, especially while out in the field where I don't have time to stare at something for hours on end.
- Fennglish: atypical word definitions, synonyms, homonyms, homophones, homographs, heteronyms, heterography, and any other linguistic device Forrest could pull out of his bag of tricks.
- Word pairing. The poem has three word-pairs: go/leave, tired/weak, and hear/listen. This may have just been poetic license, but it warranted close examination.
- Mirrored, reflective, or backward information. Forrest alluded to this possibility on several occasions.
- Punctuation-related. Forrest often dismissed punctuation rules, saying he didn't want to be bound by anybody else's book writing rules. Since changing the punctuation of a sentence can change the meaning of that sentence, re-punctuating sentences to eke out new meanings was a possibility I considered.
- Geography. "A comprehensive knowledge of geography might help," Forrest said. But Forrest also said that specialized knowledge was not necessary. The specialized knowledge statement was perplexing. Where does one draw the line between specialized knowledge and researched knowledge? If definitions of words are important, and an uncommon definition of a common word refers to a geographical feature, is it specialized knowledge if I open up a dictionary and look it up? I left that headache for another day.

Looking back after the chase has ended, by my count, the poem employs upwards of ten distinct encoding techniques. That may sound like a lot, but the result is still a straightforward solution once understood. Being prepared for the poem to morph from one clue-encoding method to another, and having a list of possible methods to look out for, made a world of difference.

Tall Tales & Flights of Fancy

Contradictions do not exist. Whenever you think you are facing a contradiction, check your premises. You will find that one of them is wrong.

Ayn Rand

"ALL OF THE stories that mingle among these pages are as true to history as one man can average out the truth, considering the fact that one of my natural instincts is to embellish just a little." That is the first sentence of *The Thrill of the Chase*. From the beginning, Forrest implied that what he wrote should be examined in full. This opening sentence also serves as a fundamental guide for navigating the book. The phrase "average out the truth" suggests that some stories might be less true than others.

"Non-fiction writers don't have to be right but eighty-five percent of the time..." was another quote from Forrest's first memoir. Was *The Thrill of the Chase* a non-fiction book? Was it a memoir that contained a game or a game that contained a memoir? Was Forrest a non-fiction writer? Was there something else buried in Forrest's eighty-five percent statement?

Also from *The Thrill of the Chase*, Forrest shared this piece of advice that he attributed to his father: "What we have learned is that you should always tell the truth, but you should not always tell all of the truth." And in one of Forrest's later scrapbooks, he wrote, "Why do we arbitrarily believe things that we've been told? Just because someone said it doesn't make it true."

It's not what you say; it's what they think you say.

The question wasn't whether there were embellishments in Forrest's writings—of course there were embellishments. *Embellishments were a part of the game* and one of the methods by which Forrest disguised the hints. Part of playing the game meant finding and correctly interpreting those embellishments. *That was part of the game!*

But what about these statements from Forrest:

> "The poem is straightforward with no subterfuge in sight."
> "There's no tomfoolery in that poem. It's straightforward."
> "When I wrote that poem, I wasn't playing any games. It's straightforward."
> "Q: Are there any false clues/red herrings intentionally laid within the poem?
> FF: No sir, Mr. Hall."

Forrest's "contradictions" were like golden nuggets—they held so much information. Once I found an explanation that allowed for each part of an apparent contradiction to be true simultaneously, it was like breaking open a piñata filled with hints. It was always worth the time and effort.

However, the contradiction alluded to above was not actually a contradiction. Forrest's meaning was clear—the 24-line poem was "straightforward" with "no subterfuge in sight." Everything outside the poem was another matter. But even within the poem, "straightforward with no subterfuge in sight" did not mean that Forrest didn't attempt to conceal the clues. For my methodology, it turns out that none of this mattered.

I had, from the start, proceeded as if there was subterfuge throughout everything Forrest wrote and said—including the poem.

Even if Forrest had flat out said, "There are positively, absolutely, undeniably, and reliably no red herrings, subterfuge, or intentional deceptions in the poem, books, or elsewhere," I would have proceeded as if there were red herrings, subterfuge, and deceptions in the poem, books, and elsewhere, even if I was 100% certain he was telling the truth. There was no other way.

It was irrelevant whether Forrest had inserted red herrings. Forrest did not have a comprehensive knowledge of the search area. Neither did Forrest have any perspective other than his own from which to view his words. Forrest himself could not know whether his words could legitimately, but unintentionally, lead someone astray. Even if Forrest did not insert red (intentional) herrings, there still might be plain old unintentional herrings lurking about. From a searcher's perspective, there was no difference between the two.

While I did not think that Forrest would outright lie, I did think he might say something that he knew most people would misinterpret or take at face value when there was a deeper meaning available. Interpret a statement correctly, and you get a hint. Misinterpret it, and you get a herring. My belief that every potential hint was booby-trapped was helpful overall and contributed to the solution methodology.

This is why, when judging a potential solution, my method ignored everything outside the poem. Information outside the poem could neither add to nor subtract from the Interpretation Score of a solution—hints wouldn't help, and herrings wouldn't hurt. I still looked for hints, of course, because they might light a fire under my imagination. But as far as calculating the Interpretation Score of a solution, the only thing that mattered was the poem.

Elsewhere, Forrest admitted to intentionally inserting errors into his books to see if anyone would notice—he outright told people he did this. He seemed to get a chuckle out of these "mistakes" that people had yet to find. I took that as a nudge toward hints and was grateful for it. It reinforced the idea of questioning everything Forrest wrote and of actively seeking out those "errors."

One example of such an "error" is Forrest's attributing the following quote to Napoleon: "History is nothing more than fables agreed upon." When looking at errors like these, the first possibility I considered was that it was not intentional. Maybe Forrest just liked the quote and only did cursory research as to where it had originated. But what if Forrest was encouraging the reader to investigate further? If so, perhaps a hint lay in the original work where the saying first appeared: *The Origin of Fables* by Bernard Le Bovier de Fontenelle. Or maybe it was something as simple as Forrest guiding readers in the direction of the word "fable." Did *The Thrill of the Chase* contain any fables?

Another example: why did Forrest attribute a quote about going bald to President Eisenhower? When Forrest talked about going bald, he said, "I remembered that the same thing happened to President Eisenhower, and he explained it was because his brains were pushing his hair out." But Eisenhower never said that (that I could find). That quote is often attributed to Sir Isaac Newton. Italian politician Silvio Berlusconi apparently said something similar as well. Was Forrest hinting at something? Eisenhower? Newton? Berlusconi? Hair? Brains? A bald head? None of the above?

And another example: why did Forrest mix up the two Hemingway books, *For Whom the Bell Tolls* and *A Farewell to Arms*? Was it a suggestion to read one or both of those books or perhaps to research Hemingway? Hemingway used to fish some of the same waters in Yellowstone as Forrest. Did they ever meet?

Each new aberration found inevitably led some searchers through a "This is inaccurate; Forrest must be lying" thought process. Meanwhile, other searchers and I would be exclaiming, "Woohoo, another hint! Thank you, Forrest!" I approached it as if Forrest knew what he was doing and inserted aberrations and "errors" on purpose as a hint-delivery mechanism.

My aberrations notebook grew whenever I found a new "error" in Forrest's words. Hemingway, Eisenhower, and Napoleon all made it into my list of topics for further research. It was a long list.

Finite and Infinite Games

*What gets us into trouble is not what we don't know,
It's what we know for sure that just ain't so.*

Mark Twain

THE PLANNING necessary for what I am suggesting Forrest accomplished would take years. Indeed, it took years. Forrest said he got the idea in 1988 right after he was diagnosed with cancer. *The Thrill of the Chase* was not released until 2010, some twenty-two years later. Elsewhere, Forrest said he worked on the poem for fifteen years. Setting aside a possible hint within the discrepancy of the dates, Forrest worked on *The Thrill of the Chase* for between fifteen and twenty-two years—maybe longer. And this did not include Forrest's activities after the first memoir was published or the publishing of other memoirs full of hints. Forrest spent over three decades of his life on this endeavor. This was no ordinary treasure hunt.

To help clarify one point: when Forrest said he had spent fifteen years on the poem, I use a broader definition of the word "poem," that includes not just the twenty-four verses of the poem but everything surrounding it as well: *The Thrill of the Chase*.

Some may question how Forrest could know whether he would live long enough to see his plan come to fruition. He couldn't. I was not certain I would live long enough to complete this book, but that didn't mean I wasn't determined to see it through. That didn't mean that I wouldn't at least try to make it work. A quote from Forrest may help with this question:

"Not a day passes that I don't question myself what lies just ahead and whether or not I can make it happen like it's supposed to be."

Forrest Fenn — *The Thrill of the Chase*

I don't recall exactly how long it took to sort out all these puzzle pieces. The basics of the approach and the steps I needed to take came pretty quickly. Taking those steps and refining the methodology took a bit longer. By far, the most time was spent decoding the poem, gathering confirmers and constants, and trying to understand the hints scattered throughout Forrest's memoirs and associated reference works. It was a tedious but satisfying undertaking.

The initial game plan was to gather the raw data for every verse in the poem and feed that data into **FORREST**, the Finite Operational Rules to Rate the Estimated Strength of a Theory. **FORREST** was an objective method of rating solutions based on subjective criteria. The criteria were subjective because there was a human involved, and human opinions are synonymous with "subjective." The method was objective because all potential solutions were rated using the same scale.

I was happy with the methodology, happy with **FORREST**, and happy with the progress I was making on the clues and hints. But a disquieting thought kept working its way to the forefront of my mind: why hadn't searchers been able to make it past the second clue? This question led to another: would FORREST be able to make it past the second clue? Although I was happy with FORREST, I was having doubts.

The original plan was to have FORREST analyze all of the data for the poem at once and return with a list of potential solutions. FORREST would then grade each of those solutions and give them a Cumulative Interpretation Score. The correct solution would, hopefully, have the highest score. That was my ideal way to approach solving the poem as it would minimize cognitive bias.

I had faith in the methodology, but I couldn't shake the feeling that Forrest, the trickster, morphed the poem in such a way that FORREST, the construct, would get stuck at the second clue, or perhaps further on.

I decided to make a slight adjustment to the methodology and switch from an all-at-once approach to an iterative process. That would help with the situational problem at the second clue and let me see how FORREST performed in the real world sooner than otherwise. An iterative process increased the risk of cognitive bias, but I still had faith in my one-solution-only rule to counter that.

When new interpretations for the first several lines in the poem slowed to a trickle, I took FORREST out for a test drive. I pulled out a map, put on my waders, walked to the edge of where warm waters halt, and got my feet wet.

PART II
Chaos Theory

The Game's Afoot

When you have eliminated the impossible, whatever remains, however improbable, must be the truth.

Sir Arthur Conan Doyle

"THE FIRST CLUE in the poem is 'Begin it where warm waters halt.' That's the first clue. If you can't figure that clue out, you don't have anything." Forrest spoke variations of those words in practically every interview about the treasure hunt. In response to Forrest's continual emphasis on the significance of the first clue in the poem, this book dedicates its lengthiest chapter—the one you are now reading—to that subject.

In the "Fennology" chapter, I said that I was not going to reveal the first clue, and I'm not. But I *will* explain in detail how I went about finding the first clue, which is much more important.

An Impossible Task

Solving for "Begin it where warm waters halt" in the way implied—using the fifth verse of the poem and only the fifth verse of the poem—cannot be done. It is impossible. Forrest knew this and said as much:

Q: *You tell us that we should find "where warm waters halt" before trying to solve any of the other clues. Imagining that we haven't seen the rest of the poem, and all we have to go on is:*
 a. "begin it where warm waters halt" and
 b. "somewhere in the mountains north of Santa Fe"
 Do you think that we can confidently determine the starting place for your treasure trail?

FF: *No, if all you have to go on are those two clues you cannot proceed with confidence.*

Mysterious Writings

That a clue cannot be solved in isolation was self-evident and applied to all of the clues. Finding the correct interpretation of a clue in isolation from the rest of the poem would be nothing more than guesswork. That a guess is correct does not make it more than a guess. The difference is confidence. According to Forrest, many people found the first two clues, and none of them were confident enough to stick with it and find the third clue. They did not solve the first two clues—they guessed.

All of this just meant that I needed to use more than "where warm waters halt" to find "where warm waters halt." But everything still had to come from just the poem and a map. "Just the poem and a map" was at the core of my methodology for solving Forrest's puzzle. Even if it *might be* possible to figure out the first clue using information from outside of the poem, it *must be* possible to figure out the first clue with just the poem. This applies to every clue in the poem. It *must be* possible to solve the entire poem with the just the poem. The poem itself is the key to unlocking the poem—the poem proves the poem.

Regarding the hints, I had no issue with actively seeking hints wherever they may have been lurking. I combed over every word from Forrest in search of those hints and will soon delve into a few of them in detail. In fact, I relied on several hints as key confirmers of a solution's accuracy. However, if a potential hint pointed to a specific location, but the poem and a map—by themselves—were unable to arrive at that same location, then that interpretation of that potential hint was wrong.

While, at first glance, it might appear contradictory that I relied on information from outside the poem to confirm a poem solution, consider the following statements from Forrest:

- The treasure is located above 5,000 feet.
- The treasure is not in a graveyard.
- There isn't a human trail in very close proximity.

All of these statements are outside of the poem. Should they be ignored? If I came up with a solution that led to a graveyard next to a human trail below 5,000 feet, should I go all-in on that solution, or maybe consider alternatives?

Any interpretation of the poem that *required* more than just the poem and a map was wrong. The key word here is *required*. No interpretation of the poem *requires* the knowledge that the treasure was located above 5,000 feet. However, any interpretation that leads to a location below 5,000 feet is incorrect.

No Subterfuge in Sight

Over and over, Forrest insisted that he was not trying to fool anyone. The poem was difficult to figure out, that is true. But there were not any gotchas in those 24 verses. There was no intentional deception, no "tomfoolery." Or, as Forrest liked to say, "the poem is straightforward with no subterfuge in sight."

One example illustrating Forrest's "no subterfuge in sight" statement comes from a 2016 interview with a reporter for the New York

Times. In that interview, the reporter was talking to Forrest about where warm waters halt. The reporter, guided by a searcher, had visited a specific location in New Mexico which the searcher believed had the potential to be where warm waters halt.

Forrest seemed perturbed and asked whether the searcher had shown the reporter the warm waters. The reporter replied in the affirmative and explained why the searcher thought that this particular location fit the clue. The reasoning was that it was at the confluence of where two shallow creeks met and flowed into a river.

Forrest, even more perturbed, let slip, "There's no warm water under that bridge, I promise you."

By itself, this statement does not add much to the search for the solution to Forrest's poem. After all, water that is warm to the touch is the most obvious and straightforward interpretation of "warm waters." But this is a strong reinforcement of the two ideas that "where warm waters halt" refers to actual water and that the water must be, without question, warm to the touch.

Kids May Have an Advantage

> Q: *Do you think kids will ever find the treasure?*
>
> FF: *Do I think kids will find the treasure? You worry me a little bit. Uh, yeah, I think kids may have an advantage. Don't expect me to explain that, but sure.*
>
> 11/02/2013, Moby Dickens Bookshop

Forrest delivered a two-for-one hint special with his answer. Most searchers probably focused on the first hint: that there is a distinct reason why kids might have an edge. That likely pertained to something a child would recognize more readily than an adult. While significant, that is not the hint I want to discuss here. The second hint suggests that if children may have an advantage, then they should not inherently be at a disadvantage—beyond the obvious limitation of not being able to go boots-on-the-ground whenever and wherever they wanted. This implied that the poem was entirely solvable by children.

One minor caveat is that Forrest did not define the word "kid." Some of my neighbors, well into their 80s, refer to me as a "kid." The child to whom Forrest was speaking, however, was nine years old.

The "kids may have an advantage" hint melded well with and reinforced the "straightforward with no subterfuge in sight" statement. While the two sentiments echo each other, I believe they each add distinct layers of understanding to the poem's interpretation.

Married to a Map

Read...the poem like you were going to put an X on a map.
02/23/2016, *Mysterious Writings*

I would advise new searchers to look for the clues in my poem and try to marry them to a place on a map.
02/04/2017, *Mysterious Writings*

If you knew the geographic location of each clue, it would be a map to the treasure.
04/05/2017, *Mysterious Writings*

Look at the poem as if it were a map because it is, and like any other map, it will show you where to go if you follow its directions.
05/04/2017, *Mysterious Writings*

It looks like Forrest was trying to get a point across. The hint buried in these statements is more significant than it might at first appear: the nine clues point to specific geographic locations rather than, say, instructions. That is not to say that the poem does not also contain instructions. The clues, though, refer to specific locations.

While this may seem obvious for the first clue, "Begin it where warm waters halt," the obviousness is less apparent for the subsequent eight clues. Forrest's "married to a map" statements greatly reduced the possibilities surrounding the nature of the clues.

The nine clues not only correspond to nine geographic locations, but there is also no subterfuge surrounding any of them—the warm waters of "where warm waters halt" referred to water that was warm to the touch and was at a location where one could put a pin on a map.

One complexity arises from objects like roads and rivers. While a clue could be somewhere along a stretch of a road or a river, my methodology required a precise "pin on a map" location along that road or river in order for it to be one of the nine clues. Saying that, for example, "Where warm waters halt is along US Route 212" is, at a minimum, incomplete as a correct interpretation of the first clue. Giving a precise location along US Route 212 may or may not be correct, but at least the interpretation would be complete.

The Early Searchers

Consider the following remarks from Forrest:

> *I know they've cracked the first two and went right past the treasure chest. Several people have done that.*
> 10/23/2013, Collected Works Bookstore

> *There are several people that have deciphered the first two clues. I don't think they knew it, because they walked right on past the treasure chest.*
> 11/02/2013, Moby Dickens Bookshop

> *Searchers continue to figure the first two clues and others arrive there and don't understand the significance of where they are.*
> 12/15/2013, *DalNeitzel.com*, Forrest Gets Crazy Mail

Those who have solved the first two clues are not aware that they did.
12/15/2013, *DalNeitzel.com*, Forrest Gets Crazy Mail

Searchers have routinely revealed where they think the treasure was hidden and walked me through the process that took them on that course. That's how I know a few have identified the first two clues. Although others were at the starting point, I think their arrival was an aberration and they were oblivious to its connection with the poem.
07/01/2014, *Mysterious Writings*

I cannot tell you how many searchers have identified the first clue correctly, but certainly more than several.
03/26/2015, *Mysterious Writings*

They figure the first two clues, but they don't get the third and the fourth and they go right past the treasure chest.
5/20/2015, Julius Brighton on Vimeo

Q: *Do you expect that people will somehow know for sure once they have found the first clue?*
A: *No, many people have found the first clue but they didn't know it. Until someone finds the treasure they will not know for sure that they have discovered the first clue.*
11/02/2015, *DalNeitzel.com*, Forrest Gets Mail

There are three important takeaways from these statements:

1. Some people arrived at the first clue and suspected that it was the first clue.
2. Other people arrived at the first clue and did not suspect that it was the first clue. Note that this was speculation on Forrest's part.
3. People from both groups reported their find to Forrest.

Forrest used the terms "solved," "identified," "figured," "deciphered," "found," and "cracked," but I do not think those terms are accurate. The terms I would use are, *suspected* or *guessed*. In any case, from at least 2013, searchers had suspicions about the first two clues. Searchers likely came across the first two clues much earlier; 2013 was just the first time Forrest was widely recorded giving out this information.

So what does this tell us? First, it means that those searchers came up with the first two clues using nothing more than *The Thrill of the Chase*. *Too Far to Walk* had just come out and *Once Upon a While* was four years away. Even the scrapbooks didn't start until 2013. Everything that those searchers needed was in the poem, or at most, *The Thrill of the Chase*.

Second, during that time, there were only a handful of searchers. The chase had not gained significant attention yet. Meaning, in those early years of the chase, a large percentage of searchers had suspicions about the first two clues, and rightfully so.

This told me that the first two clues were not only obvious, they were *blazingly* obvious. They were clues that most searchers had probably considered, if only briefly. They were clues that many may have dismissed because of just how much they stood out.

The word "obvious" in relation to the first two clues became one of my constants: *If the first two clues of my solution were not obvious, they were wrong.* Likewise, if I did not feel as if my first two clues would have piqued the interest of early searchers, then again, those two clues were wrong.

This was a *massive* hint.

There is another hint that can be extracted from these quotes. Remember that, according to Forrest, one group of searchers correctly guessed the first two clues, while another group of searchers arrived at the clues' locations but failed to make the connection between the locations and the poem.

It was the searchers who *did not* connect the dots and yet still wound up at the first clue that caught my attention.

Going back to the July 1st, 2014 post on *Mysterious Writings*, Forrest said, "Although others were at the starting point, I think their arrival was an aberration and they were oblivious to its connection with the poem."

Jackpot.

This was another *enormous* hint from Forrest: Some early searchers told Forrest where they went and, according to Forrest, those same searchers did not associate their destination with the first clue. What circumstances would lead a searcher to purposefully travel to and stop at the first clue, possibly not associate that location *with* the first clue, but proceed to tell Forrest about it?

If these searchers genuinely did not connect their destination with the first clue, what this indicated to me was that the first clue likely resided at one of the following locations:

1. A place that Forrest wrote about in *The Thrill of the Chase*.
2. A place that people visit for its own sake such as a general interest tourist destination.
3. A place unique enough that searchers would both stop at that location and inform Forrest of their visit but would not necessarily associate it with the first clue—a location that transcended the treasure hunt.

In other words, there was something particularly noteworthy about where warm waters halt. Although "particularly noteworthy" is subjective, I kept it at the forefront of my mind when considering interpretations of the first clue.

Consecutive

As previously discussed, the nine clues are not arbitrary. They share common characteristics, with the foremost being that every clue references a precise geographic location. If you had the correct interpretation of all nine clues, you would be able to put nine pins on a map. And if you were to connect the dots, from the first to the last, it would result in a navigational path that Forrest referred to as "a map to the treasure."

However, no clue in the poem can be solved in isolation. A thorough analysis of the clues' interconnections is essential to fully understand the poem, and any discussion of how to solve the clue "Begin it where warm waters halt" would be pointless without at least touching on this subject.

So if "Begin it where warm waters halt" is the first clue, where in the poem is the second clue? The most straightforward answer is, "right after the first clue," but that was not guaranteed. Although Forrest said that there was no subterfuge in his poem, I would not call it subterfuge if he had mixed up the clues in order to make the chase more challenging. Fortunately, that was not the case as these quotes from Forrest show:

> *There are nine clues in the poem, and the clues are in consecutive order.*
> 05/13/2011, Report From Santa Fe with Lorene Mills

> *You should start with the first clue and follow the others consecutively to the treasure.*
> 12/11/2014, *Mysterious Writings*

> *You should start with the first clue and then solve the other eight in order.*
> 02/18/2017, Forrest Gets Mail #13 - DalNeitzal.com

> *Go to the first clue, and then the clues are consecutive after that.*
> 05/18/2017, Screening for "The Lure"

In light of these statements, we can confidently say that the second clue is positioned after the first clue and before the third clue. That may sound remarkably obvious. Nevertheless, my intention was to decipher the poem rather than rely on guesswork, and it was essential to meticulously follow these steps in order to achieve that goal.

A Quest For The Ages

I am guessing the clues will stand for centuries. That was one of my basic premises, but the treasure chest will fall victim to geological phenomena just like everything else.

This remark from Forrest can be found toward the end of an article titled, "On the Trail of Treasure in the Rocky Mountains," published January 19, 2015 on the website *EarthMagazine.org*.

Although Forrest often spoke of his vision for the chase to last 1,000 years or more, let's consider a conservative estimate of 300 years. Barring unforeseen circumstances, the clues should stand for at least 300 years. This was one of the many benchmarks against which I assessed the interpretations of clues.

For context, consider lodgepole pine trees, whose average lifespan ranges from 100 to 200 years. With this in mind, would a carving on a lodgepole pine last 300 years when the tree itself was unlikely to last that long? Would a carving on a tree fit Forrest's expectation of a clue that would last centuries, or his ambitious hope of a chase that spanned a millennium?

It was crucial to consider the longevity of each clue when approaching the chase. The fleeting nature of some natural elements, such as lodgepole pines, serves as a reminder. For the chase to endure the tests of time, as Forrest planned for, the clues would need to outlast the temporary nature of their surroundings.

Just the Poem and a Map

"Begin it where warm waters halt" is near universally accepted as the first clue in the poem. Forrest saw to that. Even without Forrest's prodding, it would be reasonable to conclude that "Begin it where warm waters halt" was the place where we should begin. The poem itself suggests a starting point.

Likewise, it would be reasonable to conclude that "where warm waters halt" refers to a geographic location, that there is actual water at that location, that the water is warm to the touch, and that either the warmth or the waters come to a halt at some point.

It does not matter whether any of the above is correct. What matters is whether it would be reasonable for a searcher to arrive at those conclusions. This line of thinking, focusing on the question of reasonableness, will persist through this discussion.

Now, if a searcher did come to those conclusions, the searcher's first question would undoubtedly be, *where*? Where do those warm waters come to a halt?

Let's imagine gathering an exhaustive list of potential geographic sites within the Rocky Mountains that align with that single, simple, straightforward verse from the poem. And let's assume that the true answer exists somewhere within that list. Our challenge is to determine which specific location from that list is the correct one. How do we do that?

The problem, of course, is that our list will probably have 100,000 locations on it, if not more. Is there a way to solve for the correct location—a way to eliminate 99,999 of the locations on that list—using just the poem and a map? Yes, there is.

Both the first clue and the poem as a whole are solved by using the poem itself to eliminate possibilities. The poem proves the poem. This is a simple and intuitive method whose only requirement to succeed is tenacity. Let me explain.

Note that in this discussion, we won't be talking about which verse in the poem corresponds to which clue. We just want to marry the verses in the poem to a map.

Let's start with our 100,000 possibilities for "Begin it where warm waters halt." At the start, each of those possibilities is generously given equal weight. The probability for each possibility is the same.

The next verse in the poem is, "And take it in the canyon down." This indicates that the warm waters need to be a part of or in close proximity to a canyon. The warm waters may or may not flow down the canyon, but they probably do.

Of the 100,000 potential locations for where warm waters halt, any that are not nearby a canyon can be eliminated from consideration. I do not know how many locations that would eliminate, but probably not a lot. Let's assume around 5,000. Those 5,000 locations can be demoted to a substantially lower probability of being correct, leaving us with 95,000 potential remaining locations.

The poem itself has already started eliminating possibilities. Not by a lot, not yet, but we are just getting started.

The next step is to come up with good interpretations for the verse, "Put in below the home of Brown" and then try to marry those interpretations to a map.

So we'll do the same thing we did for "where warm waters halt." We'll go through the same motions and create an exhaustive list of every geographic location in the Rocky Mountains that fits well with our interpretations of "Put in below the home of Brown."

Let's say, after doing that, we come up with a list of an additional 100,000 locations, this time for the "Put in below the home of Brown." It may seem as if we have doubled our trouble, but the reality is far, far in the opposite direction.

The only interpretations for the "Put in below the home of Brown" that are of interest to us are:

1. Those that are touching or in close proximity to a canyon. Bonus points for canyons that have water flowing down them.
2. The canyon that touches the put in below the home of Brown must be the same canyon that touches one of the warm waters candidates.
3. The distance between where warm waters halt and the put in below the home of Brown must be "not far, but too far to walk," however you want to define that distance.
4. The put in below the home of Brown must be down the canyon from where warm waters halt, not up.

While there might be 100,000 potential locations corresponding to "Begin it where warm waters halt" and an additional 100,000 potential locations for "Put in below the home of Brown," I would wager that fewer than 1000 locations fit the second stanza of the poem as a whole. In fact, the number is likely much lower.

Even if there were a million plausible interpretations for each standalone verse in the poem, it wouldn't matter. As each verse is added for consideration, a new constraint is added and the possibilities for the correct location become fewer. And this happens *fast*.

This is what I meant when I said that the poem proves the poem. The first clue does not stand alone. The first clue is directly connected to a canyon which is directly connected to the Put in below the home of Brown which is directly connected to the rest of the poem. The deeper you go into the poem, the more the poem itself eliminates possibilities.

Although it may seem as if the poem can lead anywhere, it really can't. To understand this, all you have to do is ignore *everything* except the second stanza.

Try to solve the second stanza by itself. Aim for an exhaustive list of *high-quality* interpretations for the second stanza as a whole. Don't worry about how many clues are in the second stanza and don't try to solve the poem. The rest of the poem is a distraction. Ignore it. Concentrate solely on the second stanza. How many *high-quality* interpretations of the second stanza can you come up with?

Unless you are willing to get silly with your interpretations and say something like "where warm waters halt is clouds in the sky," or "the home of brown is the brown dirt of the earth," then the second stanza—by itself—is *extremely* limiting.

I mentioned that there are likely no more than 1,000 locations that fit well with the second stanza. That estimation is generous. The actual number is likely to be fewer than 100. But for the sake of discussion, let's assume you managed to generate 1,000 plausible locations. This would mean that the number of possibilities for the first clue has been effectively reduced from 100,000 to a mere 1,000 locations. And that's with using just the second stanza of the poem.

Every subsequent verse in the poem after the second stanza further reduces the possibilities.

If the second stanza can't lead anywhere, then the poem can't lead anywhere. It does not matter if I find a perfect interpretation for the third or the fourth stanza if I cannot provide a solid connection to the other verses in the poem. Cheating at solitaire works only when no one is watching. In Forrest's game, you've got to lay your cards on the table.

I did not start by trying to solve for the first clue by itself because that was impossible. And I was not trying to solve the entire poem at once either. I started by trying to solve for the second stanza. Until I had solid interpretations for the second stanza, there was no point in looking at the rest of the poem.

It's almost counter intuitive to think that the less information you have, the easier it is to solve the poem, but it's true (a controlled flow of information is what we're really looking for). Everything outside of the poem is a distraction from the poem. And everything outside of the second stanza is a distraction from the second stanza.

My overall strategy was to work through the verses of the poem all the while eliminating possibilities. In the end, I was betting that there would be one, and only one, high-quality solution remaining. The poem would prove the poem.

This method is not difficult and doesn't require any external resources beyond the poem and a map. In fact, it is highly probable that many searchers have employed some variation of this method. The real challenge lies in strictly adhering to the methodology. The most problematic thing about it is probably that it's boring. It's difficult to resist looking further ahead to see what's lurking around the corner. It's difficult to resist diving head-first into the middle of the poem and looking for the blaze. But that's how it has to work.

As you work your way through the poem using this method, the list of remaining high-quality interpretations narrows. With every verse of the poem, the list narrows. By the final verse, the likelihood that you're looking at Forrest's solution to the poem is close to 100%. However, and this is key, it doesn't reach 100% until you're holding the treasure chest.

This methodology fits perfectly with the quote from Forrest mentioned at the beginning of this chapter:

Q: Do you expect that people will somehow know for sure once they have found the first clue?
A: *No, many people have found the first clue but they didn't know it. Until someone finds the treasure they will not know for sure that they have discovered the first clue.*
11/02/2015, *DalNeitzel.com*, Forrest Gets Mail

There is one important qualification that needs to be mentioned. My method was specifically designed to achieve the best possible marriage between Forrest's poem and a map. But what if Forrest's own solution was not the best possible fit for the poem? Although I considered this to be unlikely, it was still a potential factor to consider. Nevertheless, I was not overly concerned due to the numerous statements Forrest made regarding confidence, including:

The person who finds the treasure will have studied the poem over and over, and thought, and analyzed, and moved with confidence. Nothing about it will be accidental.
02/04/2013, *Mysterious Writings*

When somebody finds that treasure chest, everybody's going to say, "My God! Why didn't I think of that?"
07/05/2015, *The California Sunday Magazine*

Although there was a slight chance that Forrest's solution was not the perfect match for the poem, his solution was certain to be of exceptional quality. After all, no one would exclaim, "My God! Why didn't I think of that?" for a mediocre solution. Furthermore, if my approach had the potential to discover the absolute best fit for the poem, it was equally capable of uncovering solutions that were slightly less optimal. And if that was where Forrest's solution was lurking, then I was certain I would find it.

Using just the poem and a map to decipher the poem's meaning went beyond merely solving the poem. Rather, it served as the ultimate confirmation of the correct solution, irrespective of the method employed.

The Full Monty

The strategy outlined in this chapter is neither groundbreaking nor revolutionary. In fact, it is a common problem-solving approach, and was the obvious choice for analyzing Forrest's poem.

Overlaid on top of this "constrained problem solving" or "conditional probability" approach, there was the solution grading system enforced by FORREST. FORREST minimized any potential cognitive biases I might have by assigning an impartial and dispassionate Interpretation Score to my attempts. If FORREST said my solution needed work, then my solution needed work.

Overlaid on top of FORREST were Forrest's statements of fact, many of which have been discussed. Each confirmed fact bolstered my confidence in the effectiveness of the method and the likelihood that I was on the right track.

And overlaid on top of everything was my one-solution-only rule. No matter how compelling a solution may appear, it faced the obstacle of convincing me to use my one and only chance pursuing it.

Combining these techniques into a single, comprehensive, and systematic methodology was my answer to Forrest's challenge, "I dare you to go get it."

As for the answer to the first clue? My lips remain sealed. But rest assured that the methodology is equally effective when applied in reverse.

Trust the Process

*If you don't know where you are going,
any road will take you there.*

Lewis Carroll

IN THE BEGINNING, much of my research was devoted to producing as many interpretations as possible for each verse of the poem, with a predominant focus on the second stanza. For example, one interpretation for "Begin it where warm waters halt" is a hot spring that eventually cools as it flows down its course. Another interpretation for the same verse is a lake, where the warmer waters of creeks and rivers enter into the cooler waters (relatively speaking) of a lake. I find one of those interpretations significantly more appealing than the other and their assigned Interpretation Scores reflected as much.

One interpretation for "Not far, but too far to walk" is where the direct line distance from point A to point B is negligible, perhaps a mere 100 feet. However, an obstruction such as a mountain or river prevents a direct path, forcing you to take a detour that could span up to 20 miles or more. I really like this interpretation and it brings a smile to my face. It's wrong, but I like it.

Interpretations of the verse "Put in below the home of Brown" invariably revolved around the word "Brown." Why was it capitalized? Given that Forrest spent 15 years meticulously crafting the poem, the capitalization of Brown had to be intentional. This became one of my constants. Any solution that could not explain the capitalization needed to be perfect in every other way, and even that probably wouldn't be good enough.

This portion of the research was a creative effort, an open-ended brainstorming session where imagination was key. Interpretations of one verse often inspired interpretations of others. This process proved invaluable in assembling prospective solutions.

Every new interpretation for each verse was assigned an Interpretation Score. Beginning with the interpretations having the highest scores, I attempted to marry verse interpretations with locations on a map. Certain verses, however, such as "Not far, but too far to walk," likely served an informational or directional purpose and would not themselves correspond to a geographic location.

The method worked well and quickly yielded a half dozen promising geographic locations for the verses of the second stanza. While I'm confident it could have generated another couple of dozen, I decided to first test and refine the methodology by working with those initial results.

I did not know whether any of those preliminary results would pay off and did not have any expectations that they would. My focus was on refining the methodology. Little did I know that the method had already identified the first two clues. Not only that, but those clues were from the set of interpretations with the highest Interpretation Score. The method worked.

But despite my methodology telling me to start with the set of interpretations with the highest score, that's not what I did. A different set of interpretations mapped to a place known as Brown's Hole, an old outlaw hideout in Colorado, and it was this site I chose for my initial exploration. Why? Because I had read about Brown's Hole as a kid, thought it was a neat place, knew there were other interesting places nearby, and had always wanted to visit there. Also, I felt there was a good chance that Forrest's boots had explored those grounds.

In regards to the actual solution, while the locations identified as the first two clues scored perfect Interpretation Scores and proved to be correct, nothing about them stood out as special or unique; they just happened to fit the poem and locations on a map.

On the other hand, despite its lower Interpretation Score, Brown's Hole was captivating. It was beaconing to me like a siren song, mirroring what I was unconsciously seeking, even if I didn't realize it at the time. Essentially, I had allowed cognitive bias to steer my course.

Regardless, Brown's Hole was a short but fun failure of a detour.

There's No Place Like Home

*We occasionally stumble over the truth
but most of us pick ourselves up and hurry off
as if nothing had happened.*

Winston Churchill

SEARCHERS "SEASONED IN THE SOIL" may groan when they hear the answer for "Put in below the home of Brown." Most have probably heard of it, many have considered it, and some will dismiss it and not read any further. I'm okay with that; they'll be back when everyone else is talking about being wise and finding the blaze.

Before I reveal the answer, let's define the term "put in" for those unfamiliar with it. Although it has several nautical definitions, the term "put-in" is most commonly associated with the act of launching a vessel into the water or the location where this occurs. In the context of outdoor adventures, particularly in whitewater sports such as kayaking or rafting, a put-in can refer to the starting point of a river trip.

When Forrest said, "Searchers continue to figure the first two clues," it told me that the first two clues were obvious. I was not looking for some hidden or secret location known only to Forrest. The more obvious the interpretation of the first two clues, the higher the Interpretation Score I gave them. While I noted more obscure interpretations, it was with a lowered Interpretation Score.

What, then, is the answer to "Put in below the home of Brown?" The Joe Brown Boat Launch (a put-in), located twelve miles north of Gardiner, Montana, off of U.S. Route 89 and less than a mile south of the Joe Brown Trailhead. Depending on the map, the Joe Brown Boat Launch may also be referred to as the Slip and Slide Fishing Access Site. Ironically, boats are no longer allowed to launch at the Joe Brown Boat Launch. Probably one too many accidents.

There were three reasons my focus was centered on Joe Brown's Put-in: it was obvious, the method told me to focus on it, and bananas. In case you are not familiar with what bananas have to do with *The Thrill of the Chase*, Forrest would occasionally relay this piece of advice his father once gave him:

"The train doesn't go by that banana tree but one time, so you reach as far out as you can because every banana you don't grab is a banana you'll never have."

William Marvin Fenn

Now that's a peculiar thing to say—it undeniably stood out. Forrest didn't stop there with banana hints. Forrest was hinting at bananas almost as much as pineapples.

Northeast of Joe Brown's Put-in, up Slip and Slide Creek, is a little reservoir. Google Maps won't tell you the name of that reservoir, but a good map will. Although the reservoir was just a banana-sized hint sitting on the edge of confirmation bias, it made me laugh.

The region encompassing Joe Brown's Put-in looked so tempting, it had me hearing siren songs once again. A quick look at a map showed: Slip and Slide Creek, Lion Creek, Cottonwood Creek, Dry Creek, Gold Prize Creek, Mill Creek, Sheep Creek, High Lake, High Mountain, Sphinx Mountain, Cinnabon Mountain, Shooting Star Mountain, and Paradise Valley. There are almost as many intriguing place names in that area as there are in Yellowstone. There is even a petrified forest nearby. How can a searcher look at a petrified forest nearby a potential location for the verse "From there it's no place for the meek" and not think of a petrified Forrest?

After momentarily getting sidetracked by captivating place names and potential hints, I let the method kick back in. This situation underscored the importance of adhering to my methodology, which stipulates that nothing outside of the poem can influence the Interpretation Score of a solution. Until proven otherwise, these place names had to be regarded as potential red herrings.

While I was okay with place names acting as supportive hints to reinforce a clue, the clues still needed to correspond with precise locations on a map without the assistance of any hints. I was also comfortable with the notion of a named place serving as a clue, provided that there was a clear correlation between the poem and a geographic location. And while I do believe that Forrest provided hints to the general location of Brown's Put-in, that's all they were—hints to draw the eye in.

That is a lot of words to say, "Joe Brown's Boat Launch is the put-in below the home of Brown," but there you go.

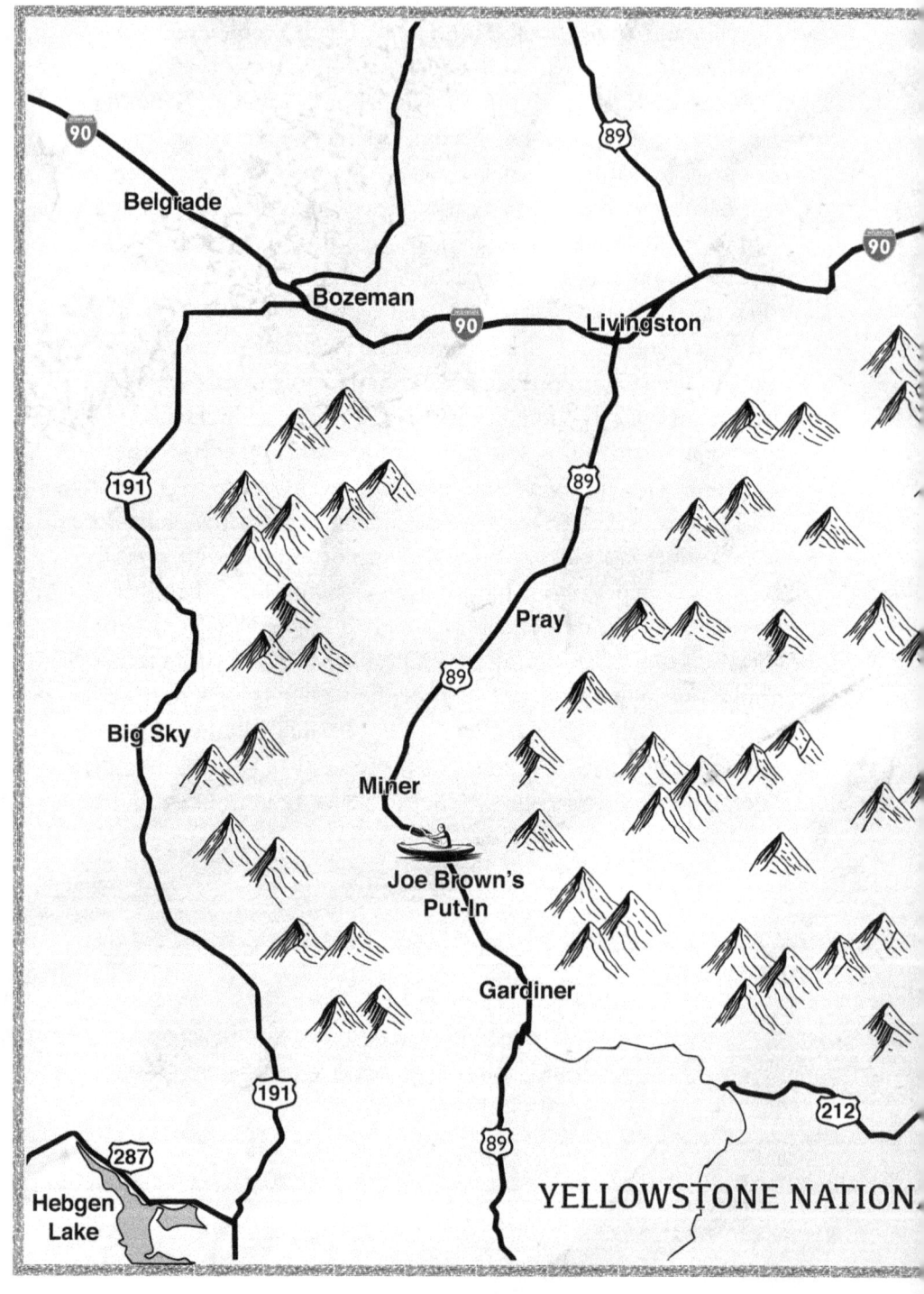

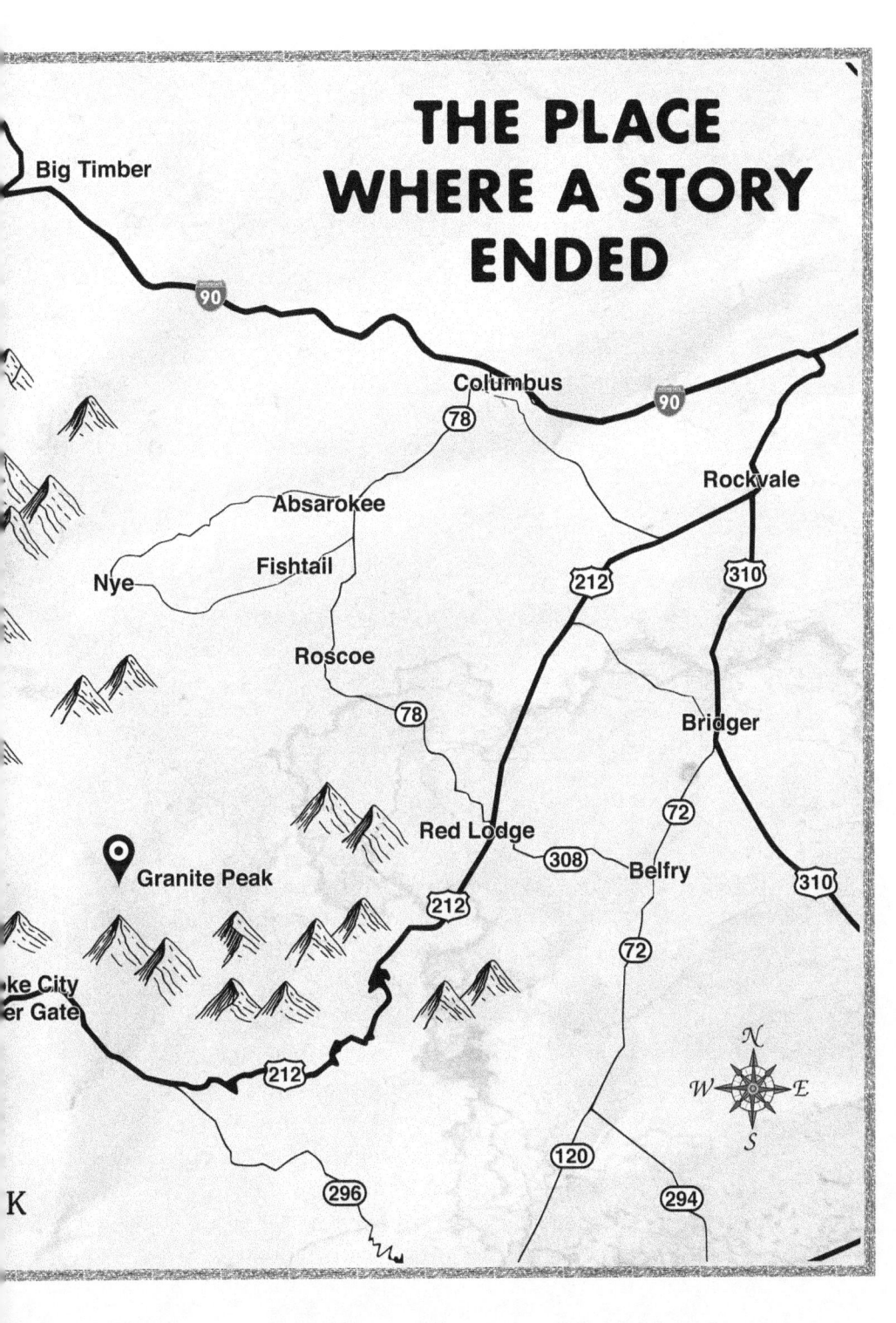

That's My Refrain

Deductive logic is tautological; there is no way to get a new truth out of it, and it manipulates false statements as readily as true ones. If you fail to remember this, it can trip you—with perfect logic. Inductive logic is much more difficult—but can produce new truths.

Robert Heinlein

PER MY METHODOLOGY, after matching viable interpretations for the verses of the second stanza with geographic locations, the process was repeated using that last verse, "Put in below the home of Brown," as a fresh starting point. Using this approach, the process iterated through the poem. During each iteration, the last deciphered verse acted as a springboard to map the subsequent verses to a location, bearing in mind that not all verses have geographic counterparts.

I neither knew nor cared whether any of the verses following "Put in below the home of Brown" were one of the nine clues. My main concerns were that they seamlessly connected to the previous verse and that they made sense on a map. My method of scoring solutions took all of this into account and would, in theory, weed out weak solutions. Indeed, the method weeded out my brief biased blunder exploring Brown's Hole.

If a verse happened to correspond to a precise location on a map, it was likely one of the clues. However, I wasn't keeping a tally of the clues. Ignoring whether a verse was a clue or not opened the possibility of winding up with fewer or more than nine verses that aligned with precise map locations. I did not have a good answer for that potential problem, but it wasn't a problem unless it occurred. On the other hand, if the method generated exactly nine clues, each linked to a distinct geographic location, it would be a strong confirmation that the solution was correct.

In the case of multiple equally viable interpretations for a verse in the poem, multiple threads would branch off in various directions, creating a web of possibilities. My method would explore each possibility and then, using the Interpretation Scoring system, proceed with the most compelling thread up to that point. Incorrect threads would eventually peter out.

The time spent on a given interpretation of a verse and looking for corresponding geographic locations was played by ear. For instance, I had devoted three full days to thoroughly exploring Brown's Hole before choosing to set it aside. In contrast, Joe Brown's Boat Launch received significantly more attention because of its considerably higher Interpretation Score, making it a more promising prospect.

At an Impasse

Obstacles cannot crush me. Every obstacle yields to stern resolve. He who is fixed to a star does not change his mind.

Leonardo da Vinci

JOE BROWN'S Boat Launch fit the poem well. It connected seamlessly to the previous verse, it was in a canyon, and it was not far—but too far to walk—from a viable "where warm waters halt." It also fit a requirement I had of the second clue: it was obvious. Nothing about it set off alarm bells in my head; it was just a mundane location that other searchers were sure to have already explored. A mundane location that other searchers were sure to have already explored? That is exactly what I was looking for—a location that other searchers were sure to have already explored, mundane or not.

By my methodology's standards, Joe Brown's Boat Launch qualified as the second clue—a precise geographic location. This meant I had arrived at the dreaded impasse of the poem. No one, to Forrest's uncertain knowledge, had made it past the second clue.

It's understandable why so many searchers had trouble navigating beyond this point. If potential third clues did not address the roadblock, then those searchers were on a wild goose chase. How many dead-ends do you confront before charting a new course?

As I contemplated the situation, I realized that the treasure hunt tested not just one's analytical skills but also patience and perseverance. Forrest had woven a path that could easily lead the eager and impatient astray. The blockade between the second and third clues felt like a deliberate design to test a searcher's mettle. Was it Forrest's way of ensuring the treasure would only be found by someone with a particular brand of tenacity?

There was something keeping searchers from getting to the third clue, and my solution had to take that into account. Not only did I have to find a workable interpretation for the verses from Joe Brown's Boat Launch to the third clue, but my methodology also required a specific and plausible explanation for the obstacle between the second and third clues. However, in a sense, this added requirement simplified the search: any interpretation for the third clue that failed to explain the problem was incorrect.

I know that Forrest implied that the first clue was the most important, but for me, it was the third clue that took top honors. I was certain I could find numerous exceptional solutions for the first three clues—provided I did not have to factor in the impasse between the second and third clues. But how many solutions could there be that had strong interpretations for the first three clues *and* a convincing explanation for the obstacle between the second and third clues? There might only be one of those.

I treated this as a learning experience. While Joe Brown's Boat Launch fit well enough, I was not married to it at the time and correct or not, it could serve as a vehicle to help brainstorm potential explanations for the bottleneck.

My plan of attack for the impasse was to mirror the approach I took for the poem's verses. Rather than seeking the sole correct answer to the puzzle, I aimed to uncover every plausible explanation, whether or not they fit with Joe Brown's Boat Launch. The question was, what obstacles, either physical or conceptual, might block a searcher's progression, from one geographic location to the next?

The inherent challenge of trying to solve the poem reminded me of a labyrinth. At every turn, a potential path beckoned, promising an exit, only to culminate in a dead-end. Forrest's design was ingeniously structured, leading searchers to retrace their steps, reevaluate their choices, and rediscover the poem from new angles.

I do not recall how long it took to discover the third clue, but it was longer than it could have been. It turns out that a little girl from India held a hint, but I was too restrictive with my definition of "primary source material" to notice.

The Little Girl from India

Two roads diverged in a wood,
and I—I took the one less traveled by,
and that has made all the difference.

Robert Frost

IN 2016, the *Mysterious Writings* website posted a Q&A session with Forrest that featured an imagined "little girl from India." This hypothetical character, fluent in English, had only the poem and a map of the US Rocky Mountains at her disposal. The question posed was whether she could confidently determine the treasure's location. Forrest answered, "The little girl in India cannot get closer than the first two clues." I did not know about this Q&A until I was past the fourth clue, but I was happy with the huge confirmation it gave.

One possible interpretation of Forrest's answer is that a physical presence is needed at the site to advance past the second clue. This interpretation faces several issues, the primary one being its contradiction with one of Forrest's other statements. Paraphrasing, Forrest said that, while it was technically possible to solve all nine clues without leaving home, he thought it inconceivable that anyone could do so. This ruled out an absolute need for a physical presence —boots-on-the-ground—for everything except the final retrieval of the chest.

More than that, there is no difference between a little girl from India and a little girl from New Mexico, Colorado, Wyoming, or Montana. Who would be better equipped to travel to the location of the second clue: a little girl from India with wealthy parents or a poor redneck from Texas with a wife and twelve kids and who just lost his job?

A more plausible interpretation of the little girl from India riddle is that, because her map only covers the Rocky Mountains, the third clue is not on that map. But because she was able to identify the first two clues, it suggests that the first two clues are on that map. The poem, therefore, starts in the Rocky Mountains for the first and second clues, leaves the Rocky Mountains for the third clue, and then comes back into the Rocky Mountains sometime later.

When I read the little girl from India Q&A, I was uncertain whether my solution followed the idea of leaving and then coming back into the Rocky Mountains because I placed no restrictions on the playing field. However, upon checking a map, I discovered that my third clue was indeed outside the Rocky Mountains, and my fourth clue was back inside again. I was wearing a broad, toothy grin that day.

This interpretation also fit well with one of Forrest's "what if" hypotheticals. Forrest suggested that searchers consider the "what ifs." According to Forrest, "A hypothetical example of a 'what if' might be, what if I was looking so far ahead that I neglected to notice what was beside me." Rephrasing that hypothetical, another "what if" might be: what if I was looking so close beside me that I neglected to notice what was far ahead?

Some might argue that I am putting words in Forrest's mouth by claiming he said that. But in essence, he did. Forrest told searchers to consider the "what ifs." My rephrasing produces a "what if" that is the logical equivalent to Forrest's "what if." I believe that Forrest was instructing people on how to think, not what to think.

For those searchers who suspect that Forrest was trying to

deceive them, I believe it was quite the contrary. The little girl from India Q&A, along with Forrest's hypothetical "what if" statement, were both released in 2016. For six years, searchers had been identifying the first two clues only to hit a wall upon reaching the second. For six years, searchers believed that all the clues were relatively close together. For six years, searchers were so busy looking at what was close beside them that they neglected what was far ahead. Forrest did not need to tell searchers to look at what was close beside them—they were already doing that. That was the problem. Forrest was trying to break that cycle and get people past the second clue.

Allow me to reiterate. Forrest saw that searchers were bottlenecked at the second clue and began providing hints to guide them past that hurdle.

I have said this repeatedly and I will say it once more: Regardless of his statements to the contrary, Forrest's actions suggested he did not intend for his treasure hunt to span 1,000 years.

A River Runs Through It

I am haunted by waters.

Norman
Maclean

"FROM THERE IT'S no place for the meek" is the next line in the poem after "Put in below the home of Brown." If you ever make the trek to the Joe Brown Boat Launch, the phrase "no place for the meek" should pop into mind. The boat launch is situated on a 20-foot cliff, leading from the parking lot down to the Yellowstone River. I doubt many people launch boats from there.

From Joe Brown's Boat Launch, it's no place for the meek. "No place for the meek" is a boat ride down the Yellowstone River starting at the Joe Brown Put-in. *Beginning at "where warm waters halt," the entire route of the poem is a literal trip down a river from the first clue and then up a creek to the last clue.*

Although not required, you could put a boat into the water at the second clue and take a ride down the Yellowstone River toward "The end is ever drawing nigh"—the beginning of the third clue.

"No place for the meek" is a connecting verse like "take it in the canyon down" and is not the third clue.

The obstacle searchers were coming up against was the distance between the second and third clues. One hundred thirty river miles from Joe Brown's Put-in is the confluence of the Yellowstone and Stillwater Rivers, just west of Columbus, Montana. The Stillwater River flows down from the mountains southwest of Columbus and through the town of Nye. From Nye, it continues northeast, passes just north of the town of Absarokee, and then on to where it meets the Yellowstone River. Forrest's poem takes the reader on a boat trip downriver on the Yellowstone River to this confluence and then upriver on the Stillwater River toward the town of Nye.

The end [of the boat trip] is ever drawing [toward the town of] Nye. Although there are several items of note near where the Stillwater River passes through the town of Nye, including what looks like a giant "F" carved into the treescape, that's not where the poem leads. The poem leads up a creek, not up a river.

The boat trip ends at the juncture of the Stillwater River and Rosebud Creek, represented in the poem by the line, "There'll be no paddle up your creek." This verse pinpoints the geographic location of the third clue, although the town of Nye could also serve as the third clue and might reflect Forrest's original intention.

Incidentally, neither Absarokee, Columbus, nor Nye appear on Forrest's map of the Rocky Mountains, as outlined in his second memoir.

Searchers could not get past the second clue because they were so busy looking at what was close beside them that they neglected what was far ahead. They were not looking at the big picture.

I knew about neither the little girl from India nor Forrest's "consider the what ifs" suggestion when I pieced this together. I was looking for an explanation for the obstacle between the second and third clues and was happy with what I found. I was also encouraged by the poem following the Yellowstone River for so long. The next line in the poem was, "There'll be no paddle up your creek," so at the time it seemed as if following a course of water would continue.

The idea that the poem would trace a waterway from the first clue to the last was unexpected, yet it somehow felt right.

Forrest provided a few hints that reinforce the above interpretation of the verse, "From there it's no place for the meek" as well as the long trip down the Yellowstone River.

One of those hints is related to the book, *Journal of a Trapper* by Osborne Russell. Forrest seemed quite taken with *Journal of a Trapper*, saying that he had read that book 12 times. In chapter 12, Russell describes his journey from Yellowstone through where Gardiner now sits, following the Yellowstone River north and then east to Rosebud Creek. Russell then heads about 30 miles further east to Rock Creek and the Clarks Fork of the Yellowstone River, somewhere between the current towns of Bridger and Rockvale. There, he meets "Major Meek" and listens to his harrowing tale about being ambushed by a band of Blackfeet Indians. Russell spends just over three weeks in that area before heading back west, where "The trappers scattered out in every direction to hunt beaver on the branches of the Rosebud."

Later, I'll circle back to explain the connection between "no place for the meek" and "No Place for Biddies," a chapter in *The Thrill of the Chase*.

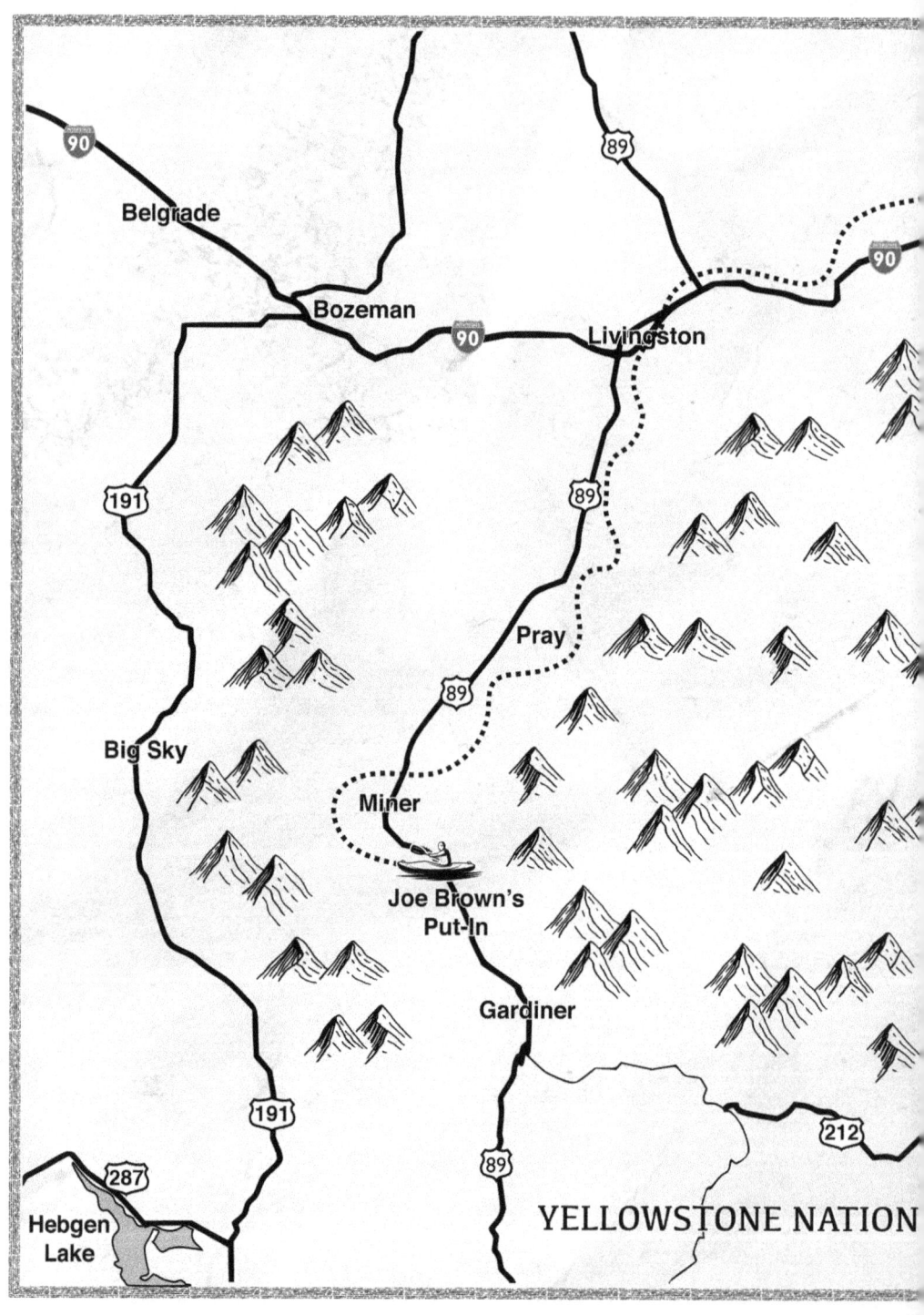

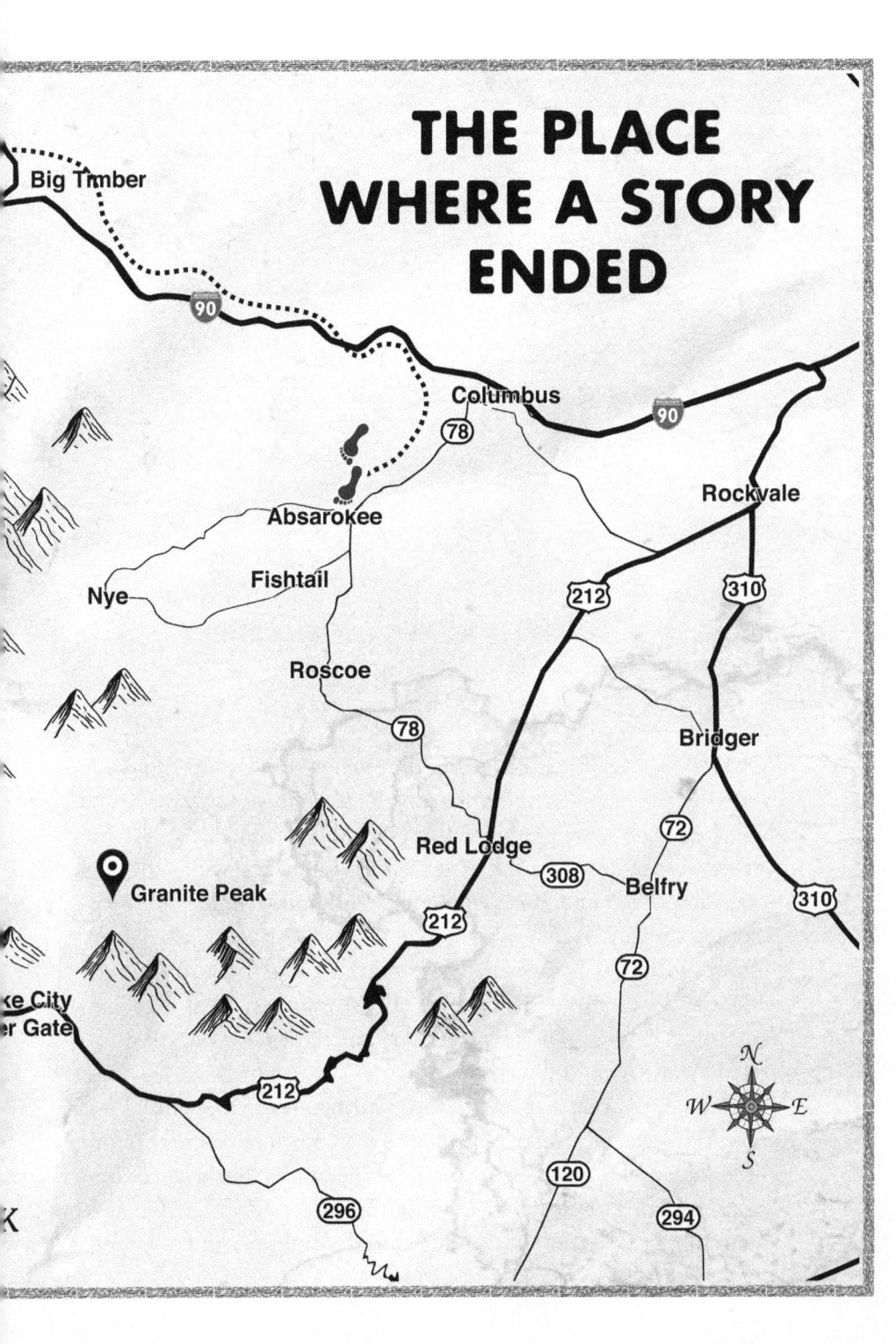

THE PLACE WHERE A STORY ENDED

Flaming Flowers that Brightly Blaze

And the fire and the rose are one.

T. S. Eliot

FROM THE CONFLUENCE of the Yellowstone and Stillwater Rivers, the poem traces the Stillwater River, and draws toward the town of Nye. About 13 miles from the Yellowstone River, at the town of Absarokee, the Stillwater River intersects with Rosebud Creek. Absarokee and Rosebud should be familiar names to deep-thinking treasure searchers.

Rosebud Creek is formed where the East and West forks come together, two to three miles south of Absarokee. East Rosebud Creek might have a part to play later, but right now we are interested in West Rosebud Creek.

From late summer through early spring, both East and West Rosebud Creeks are fast and shallow. As spring transitions into summer, the melting winter snows cause the creeks to transform into a raging torrent forty feet wide and four feet deep. Rosebud Creek is a mountain creek, not a tranquil brook lazily winding its way through a meadow. Regardless of the season, paddling up that creek is not an option.

Thirty miles up the road following West Rosebud Creek, just past Emerald Lake and West Rosebud Lake, is the parking lot for the Mystic Lake Trailhead (also referred to as the West Rosebud Creek Trailhead). From the trailhead, it's about 1,700 feet to the fourth clue—"heavy loads and water high"—and another 3 miles to the shores of Mystic Lake.

Like the 130-mile voyage down the Yellowstone River from Joe Brown's Put-in, the 42-mile journey up the Stillwater River and West Rosebud Creek is one where looking far ahead and at the big picture would be beneficial. The poem tightens up after reaching "heavy loads and water high," and the remaining clues are within walking distance.

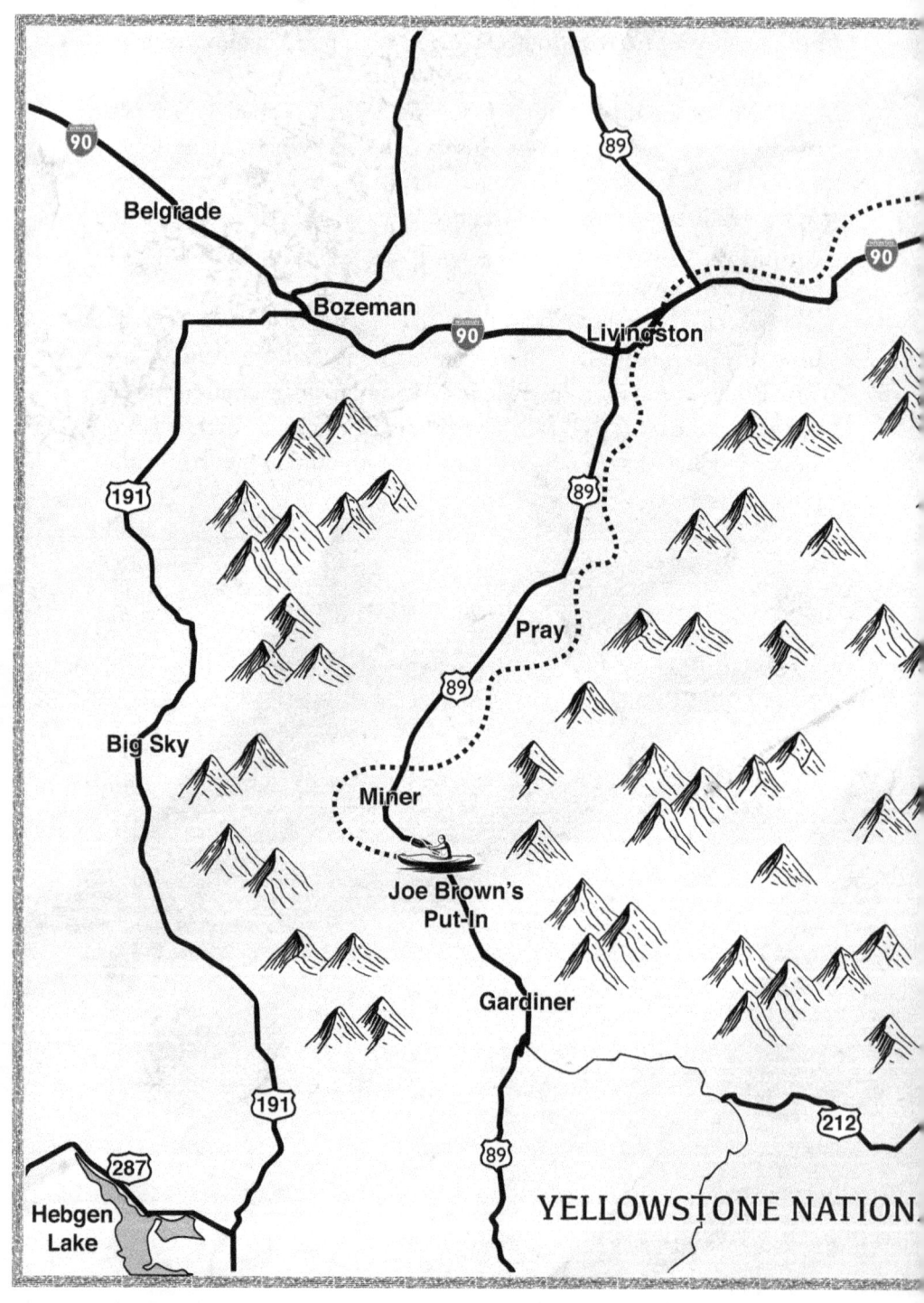

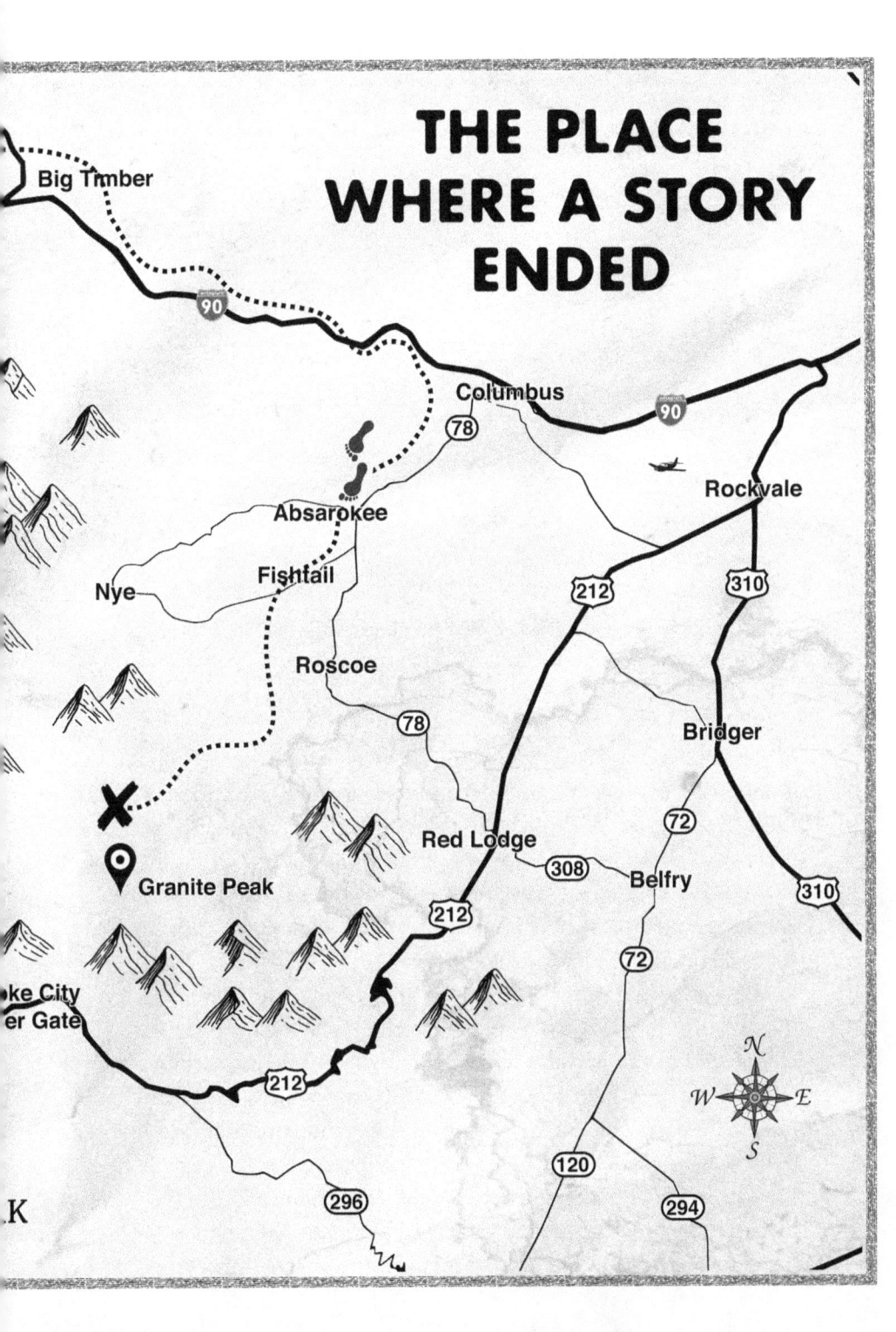

My Secret Where

In my solitude, it haunts me with memories of days gone by.

Forrest Fenn

MYSTIC LAKE WAS a natural body of water until 1925. That year, a concrete dam was completed and transformed it into the Mystic Lake Hydroelectric Project. A 5-foot diameter pipe draws water from the lake across 9,000 feet of mountainside to a surge tank above the powerhouse. The surge tank, which sits like a bowl at the end of a smoking pipe, channels the water, which then drops 1,100 vertical feet to the powerhouse.

One interpretation I considered for "heavy loads" was electricity, and the powerhouse was in the right place at the right time. Connected to the powerhouse, the nearly two-mile-long white water pipe across the side of the mountain was a likely candidate for "water high." The enormous pipe was also unquestioningly a blaze, but was it *the* blaze? This area was worth investigating.

The original path from the Mystic Lake trailhead used to weave through the power plant property, which not only serves as the workers' workspace but also their living quarters, given the site's remote location. In fact, several houses dot the property, making it resemble a small town.

In early 2020, a new route for hikers was established, likely in response to the disruptions caused by a constant stream of hikers passing through the workers' living and working spaces. The new trail takes hikers on a brief 1,700-foot journey above the power plant, where the trail breaks through the trees to meet a small bridge that spans over the water pipe descending from the surge tank. This new trail arrangement enhances the experience for hikers, giving them a picturesque detour, and ensures the power plant operations remain undisturbed, proving advantageous for everyone.

Tram tracks run alongside the water pipe as it ascends the mountain to the surge tank. A thick cable, originating at the powerhouse, hauls tramcars up the mountainside. This system permits workers to journey up and around the surge tank and further along the mountainside to Mystic Lake for maintenance purposes. The steep, 44-degree incline, from the power plant to the surge tank rivals the scariest of roller coasters. Unfortunately, this thrill ride is not open to the public. As of this writing, there is a 12-minute video on the Internet showcasing the tram ride from the top of the surge tank across the mountainside, and it's well worth a watch.

Seeing the powerhouse and tram brought to mind Forrest's "Buffalo Cowboys" story. Forrest, his brother Skippy, and their friend Donnie Joe went on an adventure to corral a rogue buffalo named Cody, who had strayed from Yellowstone Park and was tearing up fences seven miles west of town. Forrest lassoed Cody with a heavy boat-anchor rope and attached the other end to Skippy's front axle. Cody started to pull the car but couldn't go very fast because of the three guys inside loading it down. When Cody finally picked up some speed, he took the three "cowboys" on a wild ride. The ride ended when the car hit a small stream and "stopped with a terrible jolt." The engine went into the water, and the fan threw spray all over, making a noise like a helicopter. Meanwhile, Cody had run off with the front axle.

A quick bit of research into Mystic Lake unveiled a handful of intriguing potential confirmations. One particularly notable confirmation is that Mystic Lake's elevation varies between 7,612 feet and 7673 feet, depending on the time of year. Forrest had indicated the treasure chest was located somewhere above 5,000 feet and below 10,200 feet, and the elevation of 7,600 feet sits squarely in the middle of this range. My attention was piqued.

I was aware of the creeping presence of cognitive bias, but it had yet to overtake my judgment. This location did fit a previously identified interpretation of "heavy loads and water high." More than just fitting that single verse from the poem, it seamlessly integrated with geographic interpretations of the preceding seven verses. I followed the poem's directions, went up a creek, and found myself here. And, if this was indeed the correct solution, the blaze should be nearby.

"Alright," some searchers might say, "I'll concede that this aligns with the poem. However, it seems like a rather plain and boring solution up to this point. Where's the twist, the turn, the intrigue? Nothing here reaches out and grabs you and shakes you and makes you want to drop everything, leave before daylight, and not stop till you get there." If that's the kind of solution you're looking for, keep reading.

Looking toward Mystic Lake, the water pipe, and the surge tank

The water pipe and tram tracks going up to meet the surge tank

The water pipe as it spans across the mountainside

Confidence in a Maverick

Thought and theory must precede all salutary action.
William Wordsworth

TO SAFEGUARD AGAINST COGNITIVE BIAS, I limited myself to investigating only one location in any boots-on-the-ground search. I would go all in on that one location, but if I were incorrect, my hunt for Forrest's treasure would be over. For any prospective search area, I would have to ask myself, "Do you have such unwavering confidence in this site that you are willing to stake everything on it?"

Based on the information presented so far, was I confident enough to risk everything? Of course not. The solution up to this point was straightforward, it was compelling, and it aligned well with the poem, but it was not close to enough. Until I had more substantial evidence, my search was destined to be from behind a keyboard.

This brings me back to Forrest's statement: "The person who finds the treasure will have studied the poem over and over, and thought, and analyzed, and moved with confidence. Nothing about it will be accidental." It's a mistake to isolate and act on any single one of Forrest's statements, and this one is no exception. Forrest also said that he doubted a searcher could decipher the entire poem by sitting in front of a computer.

On the surface, this appears to be a contradiction. On one hand, Forrest essentially stated that the poem could not be solved from the comfort of one's home. Yet, if the solution is incomplete, how could one have confidence in that solution? Moreover, when Forrest mentions "moved with confidence," where precisely is one confidently moving toward? The poem's end? That's unlikely, given Forrest's previous assertion.

How can these statements be reconciled? The answer is simple enough. A searcher can be confident in a general search area, even without knowing the precise end location. Elsewhere, Forrest seemed to imply that there was a physical landmark or feature—likely a clue—that must be personally observed on-site. Once this clue is found, it could offer the searcher the confidence needed to proceed to the next stage. Your actions will be driven by conviction every step of the way, and none of your movements will be accidental. You will drive to a specific parking lot and walk down a predetermined path. Although you will not be certain of what you will discover along that path, you will walk it with confidence.

The methodology that guided me to the Mystic Lake Trailhead was the foundation of my confidence. It successfully identified the first two clues, and true to the method's principles, those clues were remarkably obvious. The interpretation of the third clue aligned well with the poem, and it also clarified the bottleneck at the second clue. When the poem hinted at the presence of a creek, one was indeed nearby. A thirty-mile upstream journey from there revealed a plausible representation of "heavy loads and water high," precisely where my methodology predicted it would be.

Though the solution meshed well with the poem, I was not yet persuaded to make an on-site visit. My decision to limit myself to a single boots-on-the-ground search location was absolute and my confidence in this solution at that time was not yet enough to get me out of my chair. It was, however, enough to get me to dive head-first into a thorough analysis of the area surrounding Mystic Lake. I didn't come up for air until I had an answer.

Before moving further into the poem, let me fill you with confidence in Mystic Lake and the surrounding search area. As I've mentioned before, the poem's clues brought me to the general location, and the hints kept me there, looking for more clues. The rest of this section of the book will go over those hints in enough detail to keep you there as well.

Deep-Thinking Searcher Bonus

In a talk Forrest gave at the Moby Dickens Bookshop in Taos, New Mexico in November of 2003, Forrest remarked, "I wrote a story that's in my memoir that's called 'My War for Me.' If you don't do anything else, read that story."

In "The Philadelphia Caper" section of the "My War for Me" chapter, Forrest flew alone down the length of the Eastern Seaboard in an old T-33 Shooting Star jet trainer. He took off from Stephenville, Newfoundland and landed at Pope Field, North Carolina. Forrest mentions nine cities along the flight path: Stephenville, Boston, Providence, Hartford, New York, Philadelphia, Baltimore, Washington, and Norfolk. Nine cities—nine geographic locations. The first city, where Forrest began his trip, was in Canada. Forrest then crossed the border and proceeded to fly over each of the other eight cities in turn, all of which were in the United States.

To be fair, Forrest seemed to dismiss the Philadelphia saga, saying, "this isn't important except for the underlying mystic implications."

Tea with Olga

It is by logic that we prove, but by intuition that we discover.

Henri Poincaré

MULTIPLE THOUGHTS CONVERGED AS SOON as I encountered the area surrounding Mystic Lake and the power plant. First, of course, was the potential of the power plant and water pipe to be "heavy loads and water high." Yet, right on its heels, I considered a potential tie to Olga Zvoboda. Olga, who resided in a small casita behind the Fenn Galleries, was the central figure in the "Tea with Olga" chapter of *The Thrill of the Chase*—a chapter overflowing with aberrations that teased and tempted tortured treasure trackers.

As I studied a map of the Mystic Lake region, one particular aberration stood out. Throughout "Tea with Olga," Forrest spoke of an odd "tea drinking ritual" he had with Olga. First there was red tea, then black tea paired with Oreos, and finally, green tea, although the green tea was not with Forrest.

As aberrations go, Forrest and Olga's tea parties were as out of place as anything Forrest had written. It meant something, but the question, as always, was what? And my answer, as always, was to create a list of possibilities. At the forefront of that list was the idea that the varied tea colors symbolized distinct bodies of water, akin to the various Green Rivers and Red Rivers scattered across the United States. And as chance would have it, nestled near a prime candidate for "heavy loads and water high" lay three lakes, corresponding to the hues of green, red, and black: Emerald Lake, West Rosebud Lake, and Mystic Lake.

I can anticipate the skepticism because I too wrestled with the same doubts. The correlation to green and red tea felt indisputable, but the leap to black? One might cry confirmation bias. Nevertheless, the color black often symbolizes mystery and the arcane—reflecting the very nature of "mystic." While this link might hover on the less definitive side compared to the green and red, there remains a plausible association between Mystic Lake and black tea. Besides, Forrest did not dictate the lake names, he had to work with what was available.

The out-of-order tea colors didn't help. In the story, Forrest presented the teas as red, black, then green, whereas the lakes appeared in the order of green, red, and black. This discrepancy did not concern me, as I granted Forrest some latitude, believing he might need to tweak details in order to mask overt hints, opting for a more nuanced approach.

There were also, of course, alternative interpretations for the tea aberration. I've previously mentioned a possible link between "heavy loads" and electricity. Building on that idea, the color sequence might be a nod to an electrical resistor's color coding, where the colors red, black, and green signify the value 205.

Another interpretation could be a linkage between the tea colors and the lore surrounding kachina dolls. Forrest wrote several stories centered on kachina dolls and dance masks and both were on my list of aberrations. In the world of kachina dolls, colors carry distinct directional meanings. Namely, red symbolizes south or southeast, black denotes down, beneath, or the underworld, and green represents west or southwest.

Or perhaps the sequence of colors might be a play on universal symbolism: red conveying passion or danger, black echoing mystery or mortality, and green suggesting renewal or life.

Without a solution in hand, those were all possibilities. The possibility I was considering now, though, was the bodies of water. Although applying that interpretation to the three lakes was reasonable, it fell short of offering any concrete validation. Nor was it enough to nudge me closer to making a boots-on-the-ground trip.

And then, about a week or so later….

While researching Mystic Lake, I came across the following: The pipe that runs from the lake to the power plant does not dip down into the lake as one might expect. Instead, engineers tunneled underneath the lake through 1,000 feet of solid granite with the end of the tunnel positioned 10 feet beneath the lake bed. Explosives were then used to create an opening in the lake's bottom, which lined up with the tunnel. This allowed water to flow through the tunnel, into the pipe, and across the mountainside to the power plant.

Mystic Lake is like a giant, 3-mile long bathtub.

The correlation to "Tea with Olga" was immediate and unmistakable. Another aberration in that chapter is where Forrest went out of his way to comment on Olga's 36-inch, or 3-foot long, bathtub that "looked crowded in her bathroom." To be clear, he specified it was a tub, not a shower. Although its relevance was unclear to me at the time, Olga's bathtub made it onto my list of aberrations. And now, through the perspective of "scaled symbolism," I may have found the intent of the hint.

I have said previously that if you threw a dart at a map, I could find a hint that fits wherever the dart landed—even if the dart missed the map. So I was acutely aware of the possibility that the Mystic Lake "bathtub" and the tinted teas might just be quirks of coincidence.

However, there is a concept called "consilience," also known as the "convergence of evidence." This is the principle that evidence from different sources can "converge" on and amplify a compelling conclusion. The more bits of evidence that cluster around a single conclusion, the more credible the conclusion.

Notably, there is also a concept called "false consilience." Having multiple pieces of weak evidence does not equate to having one strong piece of evidence. Each piece of evidence must undergo its own independent assessment for reliability and validity. Weak evidence cannot contribute to the whole. This goes hand-in-hand with confirmation bias where one might cherry-pick weak evidence to support a pre-existing theory while ignoring contradictory strong evidence. This is the main reason why I felt it essential to come up with potential interpretations for the clues and hints—and then rate the strength of those clues and hints—before attempting to marry the poem to a map.

In the context of Forrest's treasure hunt, I interpreted "different sources" as the various stories in his books, scrapbooks, and interviews. For example, an explanation for the "obviousness" of the first two clues and the impasse between the second and third clues are two pieces of evidence. Explanations for the chapter "No Place for Biddies" and the little girl from India Q&A are two more. Osborne Russell's *Journal of a Trapper* is yet another. Each *high-quality* interpretation of a hint that fit a single solution—especially the big hints, like those just mentioned—added to the whole.

It was the poem itself that brought me to Mystic Lake, my methodology made sure of that. But it was this cluster of hints that I kept finding and adding to, hints with what were, in my opinion, strong interpretations, that was keeping me there. And I just added two more: the red, black, and green teas, and Olga's bathtub.

The Wizard of Oz

Pay no attention to the man behind the curtain!
The Great and Powerful Oz

The Harvey Girls

THE FIRST TIME *The Wizard of Oz* earned a mention in my aberrations notebook was while watching *The Harvey Girls*, a film about Fred Harvey's famous Harvey House waitresses. Anything that made me smile or made me say, "that's weird," earned a mention in my aberrations notebook. Well, Dorothy, the Scarecrow, and Auntie Em were all in *The Harvey Girls*, which was funny to me.

My reason for watching *The Harvey Girls* was tied to Forrest's cherished turquoise bracelet. Embellished with twenty-two turquoise beads and set in a silver band, the bracelet has a rich history. According to Forrest, Richard Wetherill, an archaeologist and explorer, first unearthed the beads in 1898 and subsequently had them made into a piece of jewelry. Forrest recounts that Wetherill later sold the bracelet to Fred Harvey, a renowned hotel mogul of his era. Sixty-four years later, Forrest managed to win the bracelet in a game of pool with Byron Harvey, an heir of Fred's. Despite his deep affection for this small token of history, Forrest ultimately chose to part with it, enshrining it within the treasure chest.

Every time Forrest told the tale—and he told it a lot—it increased the odds that there was more to the story, some underlying importance about either the bracelet, the story, or both. With its twenty-two turquoise beads and Forrest's account of acquiring it in a game of pool, one might be tempted to consider the Turquoise Pool hot spring in Yellowstone National Park. Yet, such a direct hint seemed unlikely to me.

Another possibility might relate to Forrest's occasional misspelling of Wetherill's surname. Instead of being a simple error, this might be a purposeful but subtle hint pointing toward Wetherill's two gravestones—each with different spellings for his name—located in Chaco Canyon, New Mexico. This theory gains further traction when one considers the title of a popular novel, *Two Graves*, which was intriguingly dedicated to Forrest by one of its authors.

The interpretation of the turquoise bracelet story was not a case of either/or; it could well conceal multiple hints.

My research into the bracelet led from Richard Wetherill to Fred Harvey to the Harvey House waitresses, then on to the film featuring Judy Garland. It culminated in a brief entry in my aberrations notebook regarding *The Wizard of Oz*. *The Harvey Girls* held several other potential hints, including gypsies, Brown's hotel, and more, but *The Wizard of Oz* stood out the most at that time. Back then, this was just an interesting side note, not even a blip on the radar.

Playing tag with hints, as I did in the previous paragraph, is a form of "logic" that does not instill confidence. However, at that point, I was still figuring out the rules of the game. It was crucial to remain open-minded and give at least minimal consideration to every potential hint, no matter how obscure or convoluted. After all, it's often the pieces that seem least fitting at first that eventually complete the puzzle.

Douglas Preston

Douglas Preston is a name familiar to most *Thrill of the Chase* treasure hunters. A successful author and close friend of Forrest's, Preston frequently sat alongside Forrest during interviews and even penned the foreword to Forrest's third memoir, *Once Upon a While*. In that foreword, Preston reveals Forrest's intention to leave the final clue "where they found his car: in the parking lot of the Denver Museum of Nature and Science."

Two of Preston's published books mention Forrest. The first, and more widely recognized by treasure seekers, is *The Codex*. This fictional tale, which draws inspiration from Forrest's treasure hunt, tells the story of a wealthy eccentric who decides to "take it with him" by burying himself with his treasures, setting his three sons on a quest to discover their inheritance. The sons have to crack the coded clues left behind to unearth their father's final resting place and the treasure. Intriguingly, *The Codex* was published in 2003, a good seven years before Forrest's *The Thrill of the Chase* saw the light of day.

One thing I found curious about *The Codex* is that, out of the entirety of the treasure accumulated by the father, a book, known as the Codex, stood out as the most prized item. Forrest, too, included a book—his autobiography—amidst the gold and jewels in his treasure chest. Could it be that this autobiography holds the greatest value within Forrest's treasure trove?

The second book by Preston that references Forrest, *Two Graves*, was co-authored with Lincoln Child and released in 2012. Much like *The Codex*, the bulk of its narrative unfolds within a South American jungle. What particularly stands out to treasure seekers is Preston's straightforward dedication: "Douglas Preston dedicates this book to Forrest Fenn." This dedication is nothing short of a beacon, a clarion call to searchers. By the time I discovered *Two Graves*, I didn't need it. Out of curiosity, I read the book a few months after the treasure was found. For those seeking further confirmations of the solution presented here, Preston's *Two Graves* is a goldmine.

What does all of this have to do with *The Wizard of Oz* and *The Thrill of the Chase*?

The narrative in *The Codex* is overflowing with enough potential hints to make any searcher's hint-detecting senses start to tingle. Three that may get glossed over are references to *The Wizard of Oz*. The first reference, in chapter 22, is easy to pass by. Upon a subsequent reading, however, one wonders why it was included. The second reference, in chapter 59, is somewhat peculiar and feels a bit forced. As the *Wizard of Oz* makes its third and most out-of-place appearance in chapter 78, one should sit up and take notice. In my view, the three *Wizard of Oz* mentions constitute a clear aberration. Deciphering the significance of this connection, as always, remained a challenge.

Some might understandably ask how *The Codex*, published seven years prior to *The Thrill of the Chase*, could contain relevant hints. It's important to remember that Forrest began crafting the poem and *The Thrill of the Chase* at least 15 years prior to the release of *The Codex*. What's critical to examine are not the publication dates of the books, but the periods during which they were written.

To clarify, I am not insinuating that Douglas Preston had knowledge of where Forrest stashed the treasure chest. Still, it is plausible that Forrest asked his close friend to weave a subtle reference or two into his narratives.

James Parsons

Anyone seriously pursuing Forrest Fenn's treasure should have planned on doing extensive background research on the man himself. While there may not have been enough time for such research, it should have been on the to-do list. As I delved deeper into my own investigation, the significance of the name James Parsons began to surface.

James Parsons authored *The Art Fever: Passages Through The Western Art Trade*, published in 1981, almost 30 years before *The Thrill of the Chase*. The 24th chapter, titled "The Wizard of Oz," is all about Forrest Fenn. Here, "The Wizard" represents Forrest, while "Oz" symbolizes Santa Fe. On the surface, this might not seem noteworthy as many books and articles feature Forrest. However, Parsons's book stood out because Forrest seemed to be telling searchers that *The Art Fever* contained a hint.

The Thrill of the Chase is "lousy" with aberrations and every single one of them is a potential hint. The thing with hints is that some may point forward, others backward, and still others sideward. Oftentimes, it's not easy to know where a hint is heading without a complete map of all the available data. *The Art Fever* helps complete that map.

Several prominent poems and quotes in *The Thrill of the Chase* were taken straight from *The Art Fever*. Many searchers devoted countless hours trying to decipher the relevance of those verses. I propose that the value lay not in the verses themselves, but rather that they served as a subtle nod to *The Art Fever*. By embedding those quotes in his memoir, Forrest aimed to catch the attention of anyone who had read both books. And if you were a *Thrill of the Chase* treasure searcher, you should have read both books. Given this connection, it seems Forrest was subtly directing searchers toward *The Art Fever* and, by extension, *The Wizard of Oz*.

There is ample precedent for this type of hint-delivery mechanism from Forrest, including, but not limited to:

Alice's Adventures in Wonderland
The Catcher in the Rye
A Farewell to Arms
Flywater
For Whom the Bell Tolls
The Great Gatsby
Journal of a Trapper
Kismet
The Outlaw Trail
Rubaiyat
Treasure Island

Forrest referred to all of these works within his memoirs. Like *The Art Fever*, these references—some subtle, some overt—were pointing backward to potential hints. In the case of *The Art Fever*, the hint was coincidentally about Forrest himself.

Unlike *The Codex*, which I suspect had *Wizard of Oz* hints inserted at the request of Forrest, the *Wizard of Oz* reference lying within in *The Art Fever*, a book written 30 years before Forrest's own, was just a lucky happenstance.

Elton John

In his third memoir, *Once Upon a While*, Forrest recounts a curious episode of delivering African statues to the Hollywood residence of actor Michael Douglas. While sitting in the actor's backyard admiring the view, a man with rose-colored glasses and a toothy smile nonchalantly strolled in through the back gate, sat down, and talked for a while. Only later did Forrest realize his company had been the renowned Elton John.

Just like with all of Forrest's stories, I started with the possibility that it was just a story and was unrelated to the treasure hunt. And just like with all of Forrest's stories, I pondered over any possible significance it might hold. The "toothy smile" detail potentially alluded to Elton John's popular track "Crocodile Rock," an intriguing lead considering Forrest's frequent references to alligators and crocodiles. If it turned out that there was a connection between the "toothy smile" of a crocodile and the rose-colored glasses—well, that would be something to talk about.

Reflecting on my previous research into *The Wizard of Oz*, Elton John's "Goodbye Yellow Brick Road" seemed potentially relevant. Could the lyrics harbor a concealed hint? Perhaps this was a subtle nudge towards another reference, like *The Art Fever*. Or, more likely, all of these allusions were gesturing towards something veiled within *The Wizard of Oz*.

No Place for Biddies

I read *The Thrill of the Chase* five or six times from cover to cover. With each read through, I delved more deeply and, invariably, came away with fresh revelations.

On one such occasion, while revisiting the chapter "No Place for Biddies," a connection emerged that I had previously overlooked. This came to light after my aberrations notebook contained several *Wizard of Oz*-related entries.

The chapter revolves around two meddling old women, dubbed "biddies," who were a constant thorn in Forrest's side while he was growing up in Temple, Texas. It seems there's an unwritten rule of the cosmos stating every neighborhood must contain at least one pair of biddies. Forrest's neighborhood was no exception, and the resident biddies amused themselves at young Forrest's expense.

Earlier, I had found a possible link between "No Place for Biddies" and the poem verse "No place for the meek," but the connection hadn't offered any significant insights. The link is that a synonym for biddy is "chicken," which in turn implies "meek." "No Place for Biddies" can be literally read as "No Place for the Meek," a clear and tangible connection between the two.

While contemplating several peculiar elements within the story, including that the biddies resided in a brick house (apparently this was unusual and Forrest felt the need to point it out) and that they regularly mocked Forrest for his inability to cross the street alone, all of the sudden, the dots connected:

Biddy equates to a chicken, which hints at yellow.
The biddies lived in a brick house.
The act of crossing a road.
Yellow. Brick. Road.

The poem verse, "Put in below the home of Brown" led me to the Joe Brown Boat Launch. The next verse in the poem is, "From there it's no place for the meek." Or, rephrasing, "From the Joe Brown Boat Launch, it's no place for the meek." Rephrasing again gets us, "From the Joe Brown Boat Launch, it's no place for biddies." And what does "No Place for Biddies" hint at? The Yellow Brick Road. And if one were to put-in at the Joe Brown Boat Launch, where would they put-in to? The Yellowstone River.

Yellow. Brick. Road.
Yellow. Stone. River.

To complete the translation: "From the Joe Brown Boat Launch, it's the Yellowstone River." The connection seems undeniable.

I found this connection after I had independently decided to put-in to the Yellowstone River, and it gave me a huge boost in confidence. All the pieces were falling into place.

We're Off To See the Wizard

The final piece of the Oz puzzle fell into place when I rewatched *The Wizard of Oz*. In *The Wizard of Oz*, the characters follow the Yellow Brick Road to Emerald City. In *The Thrill of the Chase*, we follow the Yellowstone River to Emerald Lake, which is just under two miles from the Mystic Lake Trailhead—the same path that Osborne Russell took in *Journal of a Trapper*.

It's hard to dismiss the overlapping elements between these narratives as mere coincidence. Such direct and specific correlations, especially when coupled with the many preceding hints, is almost like a beacon illuminating a trail. This was not just another hint; it was potentially a lighthouse guiding the way.

The Calumet of the Coteau

How doth the little crocodile
Improve his shining tail,
And pour the waters of the Nile
On every golden scale!
How cheerfully he seems to grin,
How neatly spreads his claws,
And welcomes little fishes in,
With gently smiling jaws!

Lewis Carroll

THE CROCODILE, a poem by Lewis Carroll, was one of the many passages Forrest liked to recite. Among his writings and interviews, there are numerous allusions to crocodiles, alligators, and *Alice in Wonderland*. Forrest revealed that his friend, former Wyoming Senator Alan Simpson, could recite *Alice in Wonderland* from memory. Another oft-repeated quote by Forrest was, "Don't make the alligator mad until you've crossed the river."

What, if anything, was Forrest hinting at concerning Alice, alligators, and crocodiles. Does *Alice in Wonderland* point to crocodiles, or do crocodiles suggest *Alice in Wonderland*? Both? Neither?

Osborne Russell's book, *Journal of a Trapper*, gave me a subtle nudge in the right direction. Forrest declared that he had read *Journal of a Trapper* no less than twelve times over the years. When the creator of a treasure hunt reveals his fondness for a particular book—a book that spans a portion of the search area for the treasure—stating that he read it a dozen times, how could one not be compelled to read it at least once?

Journal of a Trapper, chronicling the years 1834 through 1843, contains numerous potential hints, including the journey Forrest outlined in his poem. The part that stands out in the context of this chapter is Russell's lament over his inability to accurately depict the marvels of Yellowstone through prose. Russell, considering himself a mere journalist and not a poet, expressed his regret about leaving the picturesque valley in obscurity until it could be visited by "some more skillful admirer of the beauties of nature who may chance to stroll this way at some future period."

It was in 1884 that *The Calumet of the Coteau* was published. This was the poetic homage to the region that Russell had been yearning for. I can't help but wonder how many times Forrest read that book. I'd wager he has navigated its narrative at least once.

The Calumet of the Coteau is a book of poetry centered around Yellowstone National Park, and I recommend it. You don't have to flip through too many pages before you come to the following:

> *I SING in songs of gliding lays*
> *Of forest scenes in border days;*
> *Of rippling rills in valleys green,*
> *And mirrored hills in lakelet sheen;*
> *Of mountain-peaks begirt with snow,*
> *And flowery parks, pine-girt below;*
> *Of daring deeds of border braves,*
> *On dashing steeds, to gory graves;*
> *Of brawny breast neath painted plume,*

> *On warrior's crest, in dash to doom;*
> *Of light canoe on dashing shore,*
> *And daring crew, who'll row no more;*
> *Of goblins grim and cañons grand,*
> *And geysers spouting o'er the strand;*
> *Of Mystic Lake, of Wonder-Land.*
>
> P.W. Norris

The author, P. W. Norris, referred to Yellowstone Park as "Wonder-Land." When he mentions Mystic Lake, Norris is talking about Yellowstone Lake. The above is a small part of one of the poems about Mystic Lake and Wonder-Land. Reading this, I couldn't help but imagine a young Forrest Fenn in Wonder-Land.

Could Forrest's *Alice in Wonderland* references be pointing to *The Calumet of the Coteau*? Sure they could. However, if it merely hinted at Yellowstone, it wouldn't be of much help. Given Forrest's chapter "In Love with Yellowstone," and the numerous tales he recounted about spending his summers there, Yellowstone was already a primary consideration for many treasure seekers. There was no need for such a subtle hint about Yellowstone when Forrest was shouting about it from the rooftops.

While Norris's reference to Mystic Lake corresponds to Yellowstone Lake, could there be a connection to the Mystic Lake located 54 miles away—the one where Forrest's poem seemed to be leading? Consider this excerpt from another poem that Forrest frequently recited:

> *We shall not cease from exploration*
> *And the end of all our exploring*
> *Will be to arrive where we started*
> *And know the place for the first time.*
>
> T.S. Eliot

"To arrive where we started and know the place for the first time." Did the poem lead from "Mystic Lake" to Mystic Lake?

The Calumet of the Coteau, by the way, translates to "The peace pipe of the hillside."

Pioneers of a Different Sort

*They do not know that it is the chase,
and not the quarry, which they seek.*

Blaise Pascal

"LOOKING FOR LEWIS AND CLARK," a chapter in *The Thrill of the Chase*, might more fittingly bear the title "Looking for Osborne Russell." This chapter depicts an excursion undertaken by Forrest and his friend, Donnie Joe, into the mountains north of Hebgen Lake, Montana. Forrest had set out to trace the steps of Lewis and Clark, with his friend Donnie Joe in tow for company. The thing is, Lewis and Clark were never near that area, but Osborne Russell was. Had Forrest genuinely intended to follow the trail of Lewis and Clark, he would have journeyed northward from Gardiner, Montana, following the path of the Yellowstone River.

Toward the end of the chapter, after Forrest and Donnie had gotten themselves thoroughly lost, Forrest notes, "So I applied some mountain man wisdom to the situation. The sun comes up in the east and we thought out was south so that made it easy, except that south was over the highest mountain we'd ever seen." There are a few potential hints buried in these words. The phrase "The sun comes up in the east" might suggest that "The blaze lies to our east." And, if one can determine their specific location, they would thus determine the direction to the blaze. The reference to "mountain man wisdom" enhances this interpretation by associating the terms "wise" and "blaze." This association echoes the line from the poem, "If you've been wise and found the blaze." This interpretation is further reinforced considering that in the story's original publication in the Bozeman Daily Chronicle in 2008, "mountain man wisdom" was presented as "mountain man logic." Both "wisdom" and "logic" fit well with the story, but only one of them fits well with the poem.

Another thing that strengthened the above interpretation is that the "sun comes up in the east" portion is not needed. "We thought out was south" works fine by itself. One might argue this was merely a flourish of Forrest's writing style. That could be. Although some might dismiss all of this as confirmation bias, this interpretation holds up when you consider the rest of the story.

The latter part of the quote, "We thought out was south so that made it easy, except that south was over the highest mountain we'd ever seen," brings everything together. Forrest and Donnie found themselves at a location north of an extremely high mountain. There are many high mountains in the Rockies, but this one was special. This was the highest mountain they had ever seen.

An obvious path for investigation was the highest mountain in each of the four search states:

> Mount Elbert in Colorado
> Granite Peak in Montana
> Wheeler Peak in New Mexico
> Gannett Peak in Wyoming

If Forrest was referring to one of these mountains, it would constitute an enormous hint. The precise location relative to the mountain was still in question, but it was presumably within eyesight. Mount Elbert, as the highest point in the Rocky Mountains, gave a possible nod toward Colorado.

Forrest made a similar but indirect reference to another high mountain in his second memoir, *Too Far to Walk*. In that book, Forrest talked about going deer hunting near White Horse Canyon, west of Williams, Arizona. His hunting partner was "Andy Andersen," a fighter gunnery school instructor out of Luke Air Force Base. Andy's "call sign in the air was Stogy, and he had a zest for the chase."

There are a couple of factual errors in that story. White Horse Canyon is, in reality, located east of Williams, not west as Forrest claimed. This discrepancy could either be an innocent mistake or an intentional error planted by Forrest to highlight an underlying hint. Forrest bragged about deliberately inserting errors in his books, although his motivation for doing so remained a mystery, beyond, "to see if anyone would notice."

A possible purpose behind this particular error was made clear after recalling the "highest mountain" quote in the "Looking for Lewis and Clark" chapter. White Horse Canyon lies approximately 5.4 miles directly north of Humphreys Peak, which is the highest peak in Arizona. Comparatively, the western shore of Mystic Lake is about 4 miles directly north of Granite Peak, the highest peak in Montana. The connection forms an intriguing echo to the phrase, "...south was over the highest mountain we'd ever seen."

If this line of thought holds, it positions the poem verse, "If you've been wise and found the blaze," somewhere between the Mystic Lake Trailhead parking lot and the western shore of Mystic Lake—a span of roughly six miles. Did Forrest include such a significant hint out in the open for all to see? It appears the answer is a resounding yes.

When Forrest and Donnie finally got unlost on their "Looking for Lewis and Clark" misadventure, they found themselves fifty miles from their starting point, and north of the highest mountain they had ever seen. In the preceding chapter, "The Calumet of the Coteau," I suggested that the first clue in the poem, "where warm waters halt," could be in the vicinity of Yellowstone Lake. It so happens that Yellowstone Lake is approximately fifty miles from Mystic Lake. The lines were beginning to cross.

I must clarify that I am not stating definitively that "where warm waters halt" is at Yellowstone Lake, but it might nearby. I am also not offering a specific definition of "nearby." If you are retracing steps from Mystic Lake to pinpoint "where warm waters halt," I would not interpret "fifty miles" as exactly 50.0 miles. Moreover, considering that Mystic Lake spans three miles in length, and Yellowstone Lake stretches to eighteen miles, determining precise endpoints would be a challenge.

Deep-Thinking Searcher Bonus

Recall the chapter "Tea with Olga" from *The Thrill of the Chase*. Olga Zvoboda, Forrest's neighbor, was dying, and she requested that he scatter her ashes near her father's final resting place atop Taos Mountain. When the time came, the summit of Taos Mountain seemed inaccessible. Forrest therefore chose to spread her ashes nearby, slightly below the peak. He later reflected, "I know Olga's spirit was pleased when her white bone fragments flittered through the small window and softly floated down to a place where the chamisa and mountain laurels were blooming, and chipmunks scurried around all year."

The "Tea with Olga" chapter carries a few puzzles of its own, one of which involves an uncertainty regarding Taos Mountain—it appears that such a mountain may not exist. A search on Google for "Taos Mountain, New Mexico" tends to return results related to Taos Ski Valley. This ski area lies a couple of miles north of Wheeler Peak, the highest peak in New Mexico. Interestingly, Wheeler Peak was initially named Taos Peak until it was renamed in 1950.

I did encounter one assertion that locals call Pueblo Peak 'Taos Mountain," but I struggled to find corroborating sources for this claim. For reference, Pueblo Peak is roughly 6 miles southwest of Wheeler Peak. Both Pueblo Peak and Wheeler Peak are part of the

Taos Mountain Range, a subrange of the Sangre de Cristo Mountains, which is the southernmost subrange of the Rocky Mountains.

Another peculiar detail in the chapter "Tea with Olga" is that Forrest cites Taos Mountain as being 90 miles away. If we assume he is starting from Santa Fe, the distance to Wheeler Peak is about 75 statute miles (65 nautical miles), and Pueblo Peak is roughly 69 statute miles (60 nautical miles) away. Could this discrepancy be a deliberate misdirection to spotlight a hint, or is it simply an error?

I conducted a preliminary search covering a 90-mile radius (both statute and nautical) from Santa Fe Airport, and extended the same search from Wheeler Peak and Pueblo Peak, but nothing of significance caught my eye. Interestingly, there is an airport situated 90 statute miles west of Granite Peak, near Ennis, Montana. Although I intended to investigate further, I never circled back to the subject.

Both "Tea with Olga" and "I Wish I Hadn't" include an indirect reference to an area situated just north of the highest peak in a state. And now, both the poem and book led me to a location just north of Montana's highest peak, Granite Peak.

A Key Point

You can't depend on your eyes when your imagination is out of focus.

Mark Twain

JENNY KILE OPERATES the *Mysterious Writings* website, a platform dedicated to treasure hunting. It stands as one of the most reliable treasure hunting blogs, and I trusted it as a source of undistorted information from Forrest. Jenny hosts a series of interviews titled "Six Questions with..." where she interviews various individuals involved in different treasure hunts. Forrest participated in several of these interviews—all of them are worth reading, and all of them contain hints.

In the 2019 edition of "Six Questions with Forrest Fenn," Jenny asked Forrest whether the special spot where he hid the treasure would always be secure. Part of Forrest's response was, "The immediate landscape will probably remain about the same for as long as time has to go." That is an interesting answer and a significant hint that eliminates several possible treasure hiding locations, including all private property.

No doubt, many people think this alludes to Yellowstone National Park. The problem with Yellowstone in this context is the timeframe. The preservation of Yellowstone hinges entirely on its National Park designation. Can we confidently say that Yellowstone will "remain about the same" for the next 1,000 years, let alone "as long as time has to go?"

There is another area that fits Forrest's "as long as time has to go" remark quite a bit better than Yellowstone—the rugged and inhospitable Beartooth Mountains, lying just a few miles north of Yellowstone National Park. As shown in this book, the poem's path circumnavigates much of the Beartooths before making a beeline into their core near Mystic Lake. Mystic Lake is surrounded by the Absaroka-Beartooth Wilderness, a portion of the Custer Gallatin National Forest. According to *fs.usda.gov*, the Beartooth Mountains are composed of Precambrian granite and metamorphic rocks, forming some of the oldest rocks in the world:

> "These Beartooth rocks represent some of the first rocks formed after the cooling of the initially molten earth."
>
> fs.usda.gov

I imagine the Beartooth Mountains would even withstand a volcanic eruption at the Yellowstone Caldera. Do you know what would not survive a Yellowstone eruption? Yellowstone. When questioned about the treasure's survival chances in the event of a Yellowstone eruption, Forrest replied, "I doubt that a volcanic eruption under Yellowstone Lake would blow the treasure to bits, no matter the odds..." This is noteworthy since, surprisingly, some treasure hunters still think that Forrest concealed the treasure within Yellowstone National Park.

In another question from the 2019 edition of Six Questions, Jenny inquired, "Of all the flying you have done after the military, which was your favorite flight over the Rockies, as a pilot, and why?"

Forrest answered, "My favorite flights were those when I headed alone, and at 200 feet, into the teeth of the Rockies, not knowing, or caring, where I would land."

Although the workings behind Jenny Kile's "Six Questions with Forrest Fenn" remain somewhat unclear, the impression is that Forrest received the questions ahead of time, giving him sufficient space to thoughtfully craft his replies. These were not spontaneous remarks. By 2019, Forrest was well aware that treasure hunters would be diligently scrutinizing each word, seeking any glimmer of a hint. Forrest chose his words with purpose.

Jenny may have even presented Forrest with more than six questions, allowing him to cherry-pick the six that he liked the most. It is also possible that Forrest crafted both the question and the answer, but that remains in the realm of speculation.

What is not speculation is the unequivocal link between Forrest's "as long as time has to go" response and his "teeth of the Rockies" remark, given they both originate from the same Q&A series. This begs the question: was it a strategic move by Forrest to interweave these responses, thereby leaving a breadcrumb of a hint? Or, was it simply another coincidence?

Mystic Misdirection

Many men go fishing all of their lives without knowing that it is not fish they are after.

Henry David Thoreau

IN THE CHAPTER "MONTANA GOLDEN" from Forrest's third memoir, *Once Upon a While*, he recounts a hiking trip to Avalanche Lake to fish for golden trout. Located above Earthquake Lake, Avalanche Lake is roughly 23 miles northwest of West Yellowstone. As someone with knowledge about golden trout, I found this curious because I was not aware of any golden trout in that region. In fact, according to the fishing map on my GPS, Avalanche Lake does not currently house any golden trout, although it may have held a population when Forrest visited.

Native to California, golden trout have been introduced to various states over the years. Of the four search states, golden trout are currently found only in Montana and Wyoming.. While they were introduced to Colorado and New Mexico, they appear to have since become extinct there. Within Montana, the majority of the golden trout reside in the lakes of the Beartooth Mountains.

An interesting fact about Avalanche Lake in Montana is that there are multiple Avalanche Lakes in Montana:

- Avalanche Lake above Earthquake Lake—the lake that Forrest mentions in "Montana Golden."
- Avalanche Lake in Glacier National Park.
- Avalanche Lake in the Beartooth Mountains.

What makes the Avalanche Lake in the Beartooth Mountains particularly interesting is that it is situated 2.5 miles south of Mystic Lake—strategically nestled between Mystic Lake and Granite Peak.

Another curiosity within the "Montana Golden" story is Forrest's recollection that, "To reach Avalanche Lake, I had to climb 3,000 feet over a six-mile stretch." Based on my calculations, to reach the Avalanche Lake above Earthquake Lake from the trailhead where Forrest would likely have parked, one would need to ascend 2,000 feet across roughly 4.5 miles. In comparison, reaching Avalanche Lake in the Beartooths would require a climb of 3,200 feet over six miles from the Mystic Lake Trailhead parking lot. It's worth noting that this distance is as the crow flies; there are no direct trails between these two points.

I Learned the Truth at Seventeen

> *There are some secrets which do not permit themselves to be told.*
>
> Edgar Allan Poe

THERE ARE a few numbers that Forrest repeats, refers to, alludes to, and hints at so often that failing to make a note of them should get your Forrest Fenn Treasure Searcher merit badge revoked. Seventeen is near the top of that list.

Here are some of the many direct references to seventeen:

- "In all the seventeen years at the gallery..." *Too Far to Walk*, Chapter 29. Forrest said he started his gallery in 1972 and sold the gallery to Nedra Matteucci in 1989. Nedra Matteucci says she bought the gallery in 1988. In an interview for Playboy magazine, Forrest said, "I started selling my gallery after fourteen years. It took me a year to sell it, and I sold it to my best client." To top it off, in the foreword of *Once Upon a While*, Douglas

Preston states that Forrest ran the gallery for eighteen years. Inconsistencies seem to surround that number.

- In *Too Far to Walk*, Forrest remarks, "Sometime about 1996 I started a company called the One Horse Land & Cattle Company...it's for publishing books...In the last seventeen years, we've published six books." *Too Far to Walk* was released in 2013, seventeen years after 1996. However, records show that Forrest's publishing company, "One Horse Land & Cattle Company," was incorporated in 1999, not 1996.
- "A ranch that started about seventeen miles down a little dirt road..." *Too Far to Walk*, Chapter 6.
- "Seventeen buildings make up the village complex..." *Too Far to Walk*, Chapter 40.
- "...that makes him 17th on the list to get clues from me." Scrapbook 78.
- "17th Century Spanish...." Multiple occurrences.
- "The bomb at Hiroshima was 17,000 tons." Moby Dickens Interview, 2013. Most authorities list this as 15,000 tons, with a few showing 13,000 and a few 16,000. I could find no reference for 17,000 tons.

Here are some potential indirect references to seventeen:

- If you have heard Forrest tell the story about how he got the idea to "take it with him," then you've heard the story of Forrest's friend, Ralph Lauren. Forrest never missed an opportunity to mention Ralph. Ralph Lauren owns a 17,000 square foot mansion built in 1919, and according to ralphlauren.com, a 17,000-acre ranch in Ridgway, Colorado.
- In an old interview, Douglas Preston told a reporter about Forrest's plan to leave the final clue where he parked his car at Northern Arizona University. In *Once Upon a While*, the location changed to The Denver Museum of Nature and Science. NAU borders Interstate

17. The Denver Museum borders 17th Avenue. I believe the reason for the change is that the parking lot for the Denver Museum is off of 22nd Avenue. If 17 is near the top of Forrest's favorite numbers, 22 is at the top. Changing the location from NAU to The Denver Museum gave Forrest two hints for the price of one.
- Forrest added a new story to the revised edition of *Once Upon a While*. The added chapter is about baseball legend Dizzy Dean. Dizzy Dean was born on January 16, 1910, died on July 17, 1974, his player number was 17, and he set a record by striking out 17 batters in a single game.

This could be brushed off as frequency bias, but the consistent and varied mentions across different stories suggest a deliberate emphasis on the number.

Seventeen Dollars a Square Inch

There are many more instances that hint at the potential significance of the number 17, but the most notable is Forrest's book, *Seventeen Dollars a Square Inch*, published in 2007. Material from this book appears in various scrapbooks, and a chapter by the same title is included in Forrest's second memoir, *Too Far to Walk*.

Seventeen Dollars a Square Inch is Forrest's homage to his good friend, Eric Sloane. From the Preface:

"The purpose of this book is to publish the last written words of a man who was a mentor to me late in my life, and whose memory occupies a special spot in a warm corner of my mind where only the fondest of recollections are allowed. This belated effort fulfills a promise I made to him, and him to me."

Forrest Fenn – Seventeen Dollars a Square Inch

Among other accomplishments, Eric was a celebrated artist whose work Forrest sold through The Fenn Galleries. Those who have visited the National Air and Space Museum likely have encountered Eric Sloane's art. And, if you have read *The Thrill of the Chase*, you did not have to read far before finding a mention of Eric.

During a lunch meeting between the two men, Forrest shared that he was selling Eric's paintings for $17 a square inch. Displeased with his art being treated as a commodity, Eric took over the pricing responsibilities. However, after his brief foray into business led to a thinner wallet, Eric returned the pricing duties to Forrest.

According to Forrest, he was selling Eric's paintings for $22.50 a square inch shortly thereafter, and by 2007, twenty-two years after Eric's passing, the paintings were fetching $81 a square inch. There is a problem with these numbers. A quick internet search suggests that they may not be entirely accurate.

According to *findartinfo.com*, the average price of Eric Sloane's paintings in the years 2004 through 2007 were as follows:

> 2004: $38 per square inch
> 2005: $15 per square inch
> 2006: $26 per square inch
> 2007: $31 per square inch

Perhaps Forrest was referring to the highest price one of Eric's paintings fetched during a given timeframe? On April 26, 2007, Eric Sloane's painting titled "Hill Farm" did sell for $81 per square inch. But this was not the most expensive transaction. On the same day, another painting by Sloane, "Autumn, Vermont," fetched $88 per square inch, and later that year, "The Milk Pail, Carter Farm" sold for $110 per square inch. Admittedly, this last sale might have occurred after the publication of *Seventeen Dollars a Square Inch*, but it still raises questions. Why wouldn't Forrest honor his friend by noting the painting that sold for $88 per square inch? Did Forrest make an error? Or did he intentionally neglect to mention the higher-priced painting? This leaves me curious about who purchased those two paintings on April 26, 2007.

While the discrepancy between $81 and $88 is noteworthy, the sale of "Taos Recollection" stands out even more. This painting sold for a staggering $290 per square inch in 2004. If the goal was to tout the value of his friend's work, why not choose the highest figure available? 'Tell the truth, but not all the truth," eh Forrest?

There are several takeaways from this story. What resonates most with me is that Forrest began planting hints well before he published *The Thrill of the Chase*. Douglas Preston's book, *The Codex*, published in 2003, serves as another example of this premeditated hint-dropping. This was no ordinary treasure hunt. It was something Forrest meticulously crafted over decades.

As a curious aside, Forrest provides a sample calculation for one of Eric's paintings: "At $17 a square inch one of his paintings...21" X 43"...would bring about $15,000." The example Forrest selected, 21" x 43", equates to 903 square inches. Multiplying 903 by 17 equals 15351. This figure is not only "about $15,000" but is also a palindrome, reflecting the same sequence of digits backwards as forwards—a recurring theme in Forrest's writings.

I'll revisit the topic of Eric Sloane later. For now, the focus remains on the number 17. Although I was aware of its importance, its precise significance eluded me at the time.

The Bullet

In the tenth chapter of *Too Far to Walk*, Forrest talks about the purchase of a 1935 Plymouth, a 6-cylinder Tudor model with the motor number PJ 320254, bought for $250 at the age of fifteen. Forrest's wife, Peggy, affectionately named the vehicle "The Bullet" because she said it was "shot."

Reversing the digits of the motor number, we get a potential latitude. The number falls within the expected range for that model year, suggesting it could indeed be an actual motor number. However, the most significant digits of the motor number are the least significant digits of the possible latitude. This means that

Forrest could have manipulated the latitude's important digits to fit a specific location he had in mind.

One problem with Forrest revealing a precise latitude or longitude is that it would make the treasure too easy to find. Even if only a latitude or only a longitude were provided, and that line directly intersected the treasure's location, the treasure hunt would still be too easy. If Forrest did incorporate a latitude or longitude, he would likely do so subtly, in a manner consistent with his other hints. It would not be a direct pointer to the treasure's location; instead, it would be a veiled nod that had the potential to lead to something worth exploring if one would only follow it. Latitude 45.2023 does just that.

While we are on the subject of reversing numbers for possible latitudes, it is worth mentioning that among the items in the treasure chest was an "Antique ladies gold dragon coat bracelet that contains 254 rubies."

A brief note on the subject of coordinates: all the coordinates referred to in this book are expressed in Decimal Degrees (DD). Google Maps, when accessed through a web browser, defaults to Decimal Degrees. Mapping systems such as Google Earth, that default to Degrees, Minutes, and Seconds (DMS) or Degrees and Decimal Minutes (DMM), will display different locations and not match my descriptions. Please adjust your coordinate system to DD as your software permits. In Google Earth, you can make this adjustment through the Preferences.

The Phantom

Latitude 45.2023 is located just south of Trail #17, also known as the Phantom Creek Trail, in the Beartooth Mountains of Montana. The Phantom Creek Trailhead is situated at 45.2081, -109.6430. Recall that Eric's paintings were selling for $17, $22.50 (rounded up to $23?), and $81 a square inch. But none of these values were real; Forrest made up the numbers to serve a purpose.

The numbers 81 and 22.5 are intrinsically linked to the number

17 via the story in *Seventeen Dollars a Square Inch*. The number 17 itself is loosely associated with latitude 45.2023 and directly associated with latitude 45.2081. Forrest even extracted this story from his book, *Seventeen Dollars a Square Inch*, and included it as a chapter in *Too Far to Walk*, perhaps trying to nudge searchers forward.

Anticipating the scrutiny of my numbers, let me save you some time. The coordinates 45.2081, -109.6430 are approximately 50 feet down the trail from the Phantom Creek Trailhead, not precisely in front of the trailhead sign. I attribute this to the complexities of identifying significant real-world numbers that Forrest could meaningfully integrate into his stories. These numbers needed to be strategically chosen so that the hint they provided could only be unearthed by investing significant time and effort. While using the number 82 instead of 81 would have resulted in a slightly more accurate latitude of the Phantom Creek Trailhead, finding an authentic instance of 82 that could be woven into the story posed a challenge. Numbers that did not have one foot in reality would make the hint stand out too much.

The Phantom Creek Trail proceeds west from the trailhead, past Shadow Lake, Lost Lake, and Phantom Lake, before turning northwest and ascending over the Froze-to-Death Plateau. After crossing the plateau, it descends to intersect Trail #19 at Mystic Lake. Deep-thinking treasure searchers may have just made one or two more connections.

X Marks the Spot

A man should look for what is,
and not for what he thinks should be.

Albert Einstein

FORREST ONCE PROCLAIMED, "The treasure is out there waiting for the person who can make all the lines cross in the right spot." The question is, did Forrest furnish sufficient hints to sketch an X on a map? The answer is yes, but it appears more like an asterisk than an X. Let me be clear, though: while the point of intersection of these lines is not far from the treasure, it does not pinpoint the exact location or correspond with any of the nine clues. Rather, it serves as a subtle suggestion, whispering, "you're in the right vicinity, maybe you should look around a bit."

I never expected Forrest to mark the exact location of the treasure with an X and would have been surprised if he had. I believed that doing so would have undoubtedly resulted in determined searchers discovering it a long time ago. Instead, identifying a nearby area that aligned with local landmarks could enable a more indirect strategy for casting an X on a map. So, where exactly is this elusive X?

In Chapter 39 of *Too Far to Walk*, Forrest talks about flying alone from Santa Fe, heading north for Colorado, Wyoming, or Montana: "My destination was not something I had to worry about for at least 600 miles." When is 600 miles not 600 miles? When it is 600 nautical miles, which is what a pilot would use. 600 nautical miles is equal to 690 statute miles and, if you measure from Santa Fe Regional Airport and draw an arc at 690 statute miles, the arc will pass just south of Mystic Lake as it intersects a 50-mile arc drawn from "where warm waters halt." Refer to the chapter "Pioneers of a Different Sort" if the relevance of this 50-mile arc is not immediately clear.

Combined with the multitude of hints clustered in the same region, this X was compelling, but it turned out to be even more so. The latitude specified in the chapter "I Learned The Truth at Seventeen" (45.2081) nearly intersects with the meeting point of the two arcs. That's both astonishing and somewhat surreal. Both 600 and 50 are *very* round numbers and they happen to converge near the same latitude as the Phantom Creek Trailhead? Okay, they might be off by a few hundred feet, but that's pretty darn close.

While writing this book, I decided to go looking for a longitude as well. Sure enough....

Over the years, Forrest frequently mentioned 109 "rules" he made for himself, starting with, "Don't make the alligator mad until you've crossed the river." Like everything else that Forrest repeated with regularity, 109 was a potential hint and there was a high probability that he was hinting at longitude 109.xxxxxx.

In the context of navigational or mapping terminology, the term "rule," as in "109 rules," can relate to longitude. "Rule" in some contexts means a straight line, and longitude lines are essentially straight lines that go from the North Pole to the South Pole on a globe. They are often used as rules or guides to establish east-west positions on the Earth's surface.

The part of the longitude after the decimal point comes from Chapter 24 of *Too Far to Walk*. There, Forrest discusses General

Douglas MacArthur and asserts that MacArthur earned, "the highest mark ever achieved at that institution," referring to West Point. That statement is incorrect. While MacArthur was first in his class, two others in prior years had higher marks. Any time Forrest makes a mistake, especially an easily avoidable mistake, it is a good idea to question why.

Admittedly, the next part may seem to epitomize confirmation bias, but I *really* wanted to find a longitudinal line running through the X.

Forrest mentions that MacArthur earned 2424.12 grade merits out of a possible 2470, which equals a 98.14% score. When overlaying 109 and 9814, the result, 109814, translates to longitude -109.814, which just so happens to intersect the "X." And that brings the number of lines crossing to four.

That longitude is less than a quarter mile west of where Forrest and Donnie would have been standing as they looked south to the highest mountain they'd ever seen—Granite Peak. It's also close to where the metaphorical alligator guards the river crossing, as explained in a later chapter.

My supporting theory is that Forrest wanted to supply this longitude as a subtle hint and sought a way to incorporate it.. Searching for variations of numbers close to 109.8xxxxx, in both forward and reverse, Forrest stumbled across MacArthur's 98.14% score from West Point and created a story around it.

While one might dismiss this as coincidence, the symbolism in the rest of that story aligns well with the surrounding landscape, bolstering this theory.

The quest to find a longitude that met the "X" on the map was more of a playful detour. You can take it or leave it, but rest assured, there are plenty more confirmations to follow.

The Omega Man

*I suppose it's like the ticking crocodile, isn't it?
Time is chasing after all of us.*

J. M. Barrie – *Peter Pan*

Ω

ABOUT 28 MILES west and roughly 1,100 feet north of the Phantom Creek Trailhead, the Omega Mine sits nestled at the approximate coordinates of 45.21122, -110.21929. You will need a good map to find it, but rest assured, it's there. Disclaimer: If you look at a satellite view of those coordinates, you will not see a mine entrance. Mining claims are typically 20 acres in size and can have more than one entrance. The coordinates are simply where my map says the mine is located.

There are numerous mines in that vicinity, including the Hidden Treasure Mine, located less than a mile north of the Omega mine. While it may be a coincidence, a part of me wonders if Forrest purchased old mine sites, or maybe staked a claim, just so that he could have naming rights. I don't know if that's something Forrest would have done, but considering the time and effort he put into this endeavor, it would not surprise me.

Before anyone goes traipsing around mines, it's crucial to remember that Forrest explicitly stated his treasure was not concealed within a mine. Additionally, these mines are situated on private property, which Forrest categorically ruled out twice. Besides, the poem does not lead there; it leads somewhere much more compelling.

Another point of interest in the general area is Omega Lake, located approximately 12 miles southeast of Mystic Lake. Again, you'll need a good map to find it.

For those unfamiliar with the relevance of the term "omega" in the context of the treasure hunt, there is an enduring mystery about omega symbols—$\Omega\Omega$—that Forrest included on the last page of some of his books. The significance of these symbols is still unclear; Forrest remained tight-lipped on the subject.

Omega symbols appear in *The Thrill of the Chase*, *Too Far to Walk*, *Once Upon a While* (revised edition only), and *Seventeen Dollars a Square Inch*. Notably, the first edition of *Once Upon a While*, which was not published by Forrest's publishing company, lacks these symbols. A solitary omega symbol is included in the revised edition of *Once Upon a While*, which *was* published by Forrest's publishing company. The remaining aforementioned books, all published by Forrest's company, contain two omega symbols each. To my knowledge, none of Forrest's books published prior to *Seventeen Dollars a Square Inch* include these symbols.

I didn't spend any time trying to decipher the meaning of the omegas; I just made a mental note should anything related cross my path while searching. Following the bulk of my research on Mystic Lake, I broadened my search area, leading to the discovery of Omega Lake, Omega Mine, and Hidden Treasure Mine. The Omega Mine, being so close to the latitude of the Phantom Creek Trailhead, was interesting, but my reaction to finding it was muted. That, however, would change.

Deep-Thinking Searcher Bonus

Despite the title of this chapter, I want to clarify that I am neither suggesting nor even remotely hinting that Forrest was the individual the media named "The Omega Man," who fabricated counterfeit double eagle coins during the 1970s. Nor am I suggesting that Forrest knew that person or had anything at all to do with the omega coins. Neither am I implying that Charlton Heston had anything to do with the chase.

I urge readers not to infer any hidden meaning in the chapter title that does not exist. I just thought it would serve as a suitable title for this chapter.

To Boldly Go

From a certain point onward there is no longer any turning back. That is the point that must be reached.

Franz Kafka

MYSTIC LAKE first appeared on my radar in late 2018. By March 2019, I had completed most of my research on the general area. I had a specific parking lot to drive to, a specific path to walk, specific locations along that path to investigate, and I was busy planning a trip.

What I didn't have was an answer for much of anything past the trailhead. Given infinite time, I would have continued researching from home until I decoded all the clues. However, I felt an urgency that I couldn't shake. Time was slipping away. If there were hints and clues in the field, I needed to know about them.

Making a boots-on-the-ground journey to Mystic Lake would invoke the self-imposed rule I had of pursuing only one solution. I was at peace with that. Everything I saw indicated this location was correct. I placed my bet and went all-in.

Trail sign on the way to Mystic Lake

West Rosebud Lake looking toward Mystic Lake

The top of the pass overlooking Mystic Lake

PART III
Consilience

Where Someone Has Gone Before

TO MAKE the journey to Mystic Lake by following the route in the poem, begin at "where warm waters halt" and make your way down to Joe Brown's Put-in, north of Gardiner, Montana. From there, follow the Yellowstone River as it parallels U.S. Route 89 north out of Gardiner. Upon reaching the town of Livingston, continue following the Yellowstone River as it meanders east and parallels Interstate 90. If you have the desire, the experience, and an extra week or so, you can make the trip in a boat. I just drove my car.

The trip down the river ends when the Yellowstone River reaches the town of Columbus, Montana. If you need to stock up on provisions, Columbus is where you want to shop if you're looking for something other than the most basic of supplies.

From Columbus, head southwest, following the Stillwater River and Highway 78, to the town of Absarokee. The town of Absarokee is a neat little Montana town and worth a visit. I particularly like the stonework construction of a couple of the old school buildings. An important note for those making the trip to the poem's destination: Absarokee is the next-to-last chance for supplies before heading into the mountains. The last chance is the Fishtail General Store seven miles away in Fishtail, Montana.

From Absarokee, follow Rosebud Creek down to Nye Road. Take Nye Road west through the little town of Fishtail, making sure to obey the drastically reduced speed limits in little Montana towns. From Fishtail, it's just under a mile to West Rosebud Road, which is off to the south of Nye Road and easy to miss.

After about six miles on West Rosebud Road, the paved road turns to dirt. The dirt road slowly grows more potholes, washboard ripples, and other hazards for the next fourteen miles as it narrows in width while winding through the foothills. The banks are steep, and this is not a drive you want to make during winter.

Along the way, you may see wildlife such as eagles, river otters, foxes, chipmunks, and sometimes a fox inviting a chipmunk to lunch. You may even see an elusive blond grizzly. You will likely see free-range cattle, which will not appreciate having to share the road with you. Be careful around them; if you break it, you bought it.

Getting closer to the destination, if you travel in early spring, you will encounter mud puddles that, if you're not careful, will derail your trip while you try to dig yourself out of a hole that can't decide whether it's filled with mud or ice. If you're lucky, someone who can lend a hand or a winch may come along in a day or two.

Near the mud puddles, off to the north side of the road, is Reeves Lake. Nearly entirely covered over with lily pads, it really should be called Lily Pad Lake. It's interesting how the lily pads survive the harsh winters and come back with more resolve in the spring. Tenacity is not one of their shortcomings.

Twenty miles after the turnoff onto West Rosebud Road, after passing Reeves Lake, Emerald Lake, West Rosebud Lake, and Chicken Creek, you will pull into the Mystic Lake Trailhead parking lot. The road continues for the Mystic Lake power plant workers, while the parking lot is the stopping point for those looking for an adventure.

Travelers originating from Cody, Wyoming, can approach from the east side of the Beartooth Mountains. To do this, navigate north using Highway 120, cruising parallel to the Clarks Fork of the Yellowstone River. Highway 120 changes its name to Highway 72 as it crosses the border into Montana. From there, you'll go north to Belfry, Montana, northwest on Highway 308 to the town of Red Lodge, then northwest on Highway 78 through the town of Roscoe to Nye Road. After that, follow the same directions from Nye Road as previously stated.

There are a few campgrounds along the route. The closest campground to the trailhead is Emerald Lake Campground, about 2 miles away. This fee-to-stay campground has toilet facilities, potable water, fire rings, picnic tables, and not much else. There are no hosts and no reservations. It's a first come, first served popular campground and, if you go on a weekend or a holiday in the summer, you probably won't be getting a spot. The Beartooth Mountains are grizzly country. If you're unfamiliar with camping in grizzly territory, figure it out before leaving home. If you can't get a campsite at Emerald Lake Campground, head back the way you came until you find a campground with an open spot or a motel with a lit "vacancy" sign.

If you are into fishing, you can catch dinner at Emerald Lake, West Rosebud Lake, or Mystic Lake, but be sure to purchase a fishing license before casting a line.

Emerald Lake Campground sign

I first made the drive following the route in the poem in early June 2019. I drove all night to get there and went straight to the trailhead without setting up camp. I had eager feet. It was early morning, just before dawn, when I arrived. I love that time of the morning, when there's a mist suspended over the waters, everything is still, and there's a new-day smell in the air. As I reached West Rosebud Lake, an Osprey had just caught breakfast and was struggling to gain altitude as it flew out of sight behind the lodgepole pines going up West Rosebud Creek. I was finally there and flying as high as the Osprey.

I am told that I should not have made that trip in June. My right shoulder was causing me extensive and unrelenting pain, even more so when I tried to sleep, which meant I was not getting much sleep. The doctor and I had different opinions about the cause of the pain. After a slew of tests, she concluded that it was inconclusive and that perhaps more tests would reveal the answer. The words "degenerative" and "old" may have been uttered. I was of the opinion that it was referred pain through a nerve. But there was not enough time to figure out who was right—I had a treasure to find.

It was cold, rainy, windy, and there was still snow on the trail during that first trip. Exploring was slow and painful. I don't know what I would have done had I found the chest—maybe carry the contents out one coin at a time. Surprisingly, trying to sleep in camp wasn't any easier than trying to sleep at home. The painkillers weren't working, the three pounds of gear I was carrying in my backpack were dragging me down, and every step was a new nightmare. But I got the information I needed. It was the best trip.

The False Blaze

LOOKING at an aerial view of the space between the Mystic Lake Trailhead and Mystic Lake, it is impossible not to notice the five-foot diameter white pipe that spans almost two miles across the mountainside and then drops 1,100 vertical feet down to the powerhouse. When asked for the definition of a "blaze," Forrest replied, "anything that stands out." The pipe not only fits that definition, but it is contiguous with (touching) heavy loads and water high. That sounds like a good candidate for Forrest's blaze, and it would be understandable if someone spent some time beneath it, scouring the area for the treasure chest.

It turns out that it doesn't matter whether the pipe is *the* blaze or just *a* blaze. Once you figure out that the verse "If you've been wise and found the blaze" is not the last clue of the poem, it doesn't matter which blaze you use—I found four—they all lead to the same location. The difference between them is that only one of the blazes tells the story. Perhaps that is why, when asked if the person solving the poem would know why the spot was special to him, Forrest replied, "maybe."

There's another blaze nearby that, while it stands out and would grab your attention if you saw it, is much subtler than a water pipe across a mountainside. The poem had, thus far, brought me to "heavy loads and water high." The next verse of the poem is, "If you've been wise and found the blaze." What is a blaze? "Anything that stands out." On the trail to Mystic Lake, less than 3/4 of a mile from the trailhead, a bronze memorial plaque is attached to a four-foot-high boulder. The plaque reads:

BSA TROUP 416
IN MEMORY OF
MARK E. VONSEGGERN
2-6-67 — 5-20-79
BE PREPARED

I was not out for a day hike when I first saw the plaque—I was in treasure hunting mode and was hypersensitive to "anything that stands out." The plaque, dedicated to the young Boy Scout, Mark Edward Von Seggern, stands out. The plaque was a blaze, but was the plaque *the* blaze?

My methodology told me that the blaze was likely somewhere west of the trailhead, so anything that stood out west of the trailhead was given serious consideration. The water pipe and the memorial plaque were two possibilities. After a few minutes of lightly exploring near the plaque, I found a third.

About fifty feet east of the memorial plaque, on the side of the trail nearest the creek, echoing the verse from the poem, "Look quickly down your quest to cease," the word "Look" is carved into an aspen tree with an arrow pointing down and toward West Rosebud Creek. The carving is on the west side of the tree and easily missed by tired hikers returning from a day full of exploring. When I first saw it, I excitedly groaned at the prospect of a phony blaze.

I was aware that Forrest shared photos of tree carvings he made—some with his initials and others of stick figures—but I was not expecting to see one here, especially one tied to the poem in such a blatant way. From the look of it, someone had carved it many years prior. Was that person Forrest? Another searcher? Was the chest found years ago? Was it just a coincidence? I had no idea.

I have never considered a carving on a tree to be a likely part of the puzzle, as it could be too easily damaged. If Forrest had carved it and a searcher recognized it, the searcher could erase it in seconds. If another searcher had carved it, then for what purpose? As a taunt? Forrest was adamant that the chest was still out there. What if someone had taken the chest, gone in peace, and hadn't bothered to tell Forrest? There were more questions than answers.

The "False Blaze"

Still, I couldn't dismiss this "false blaze" as there was a slight chance Forrest had carved it and that it was necessary for the correct solution. There was also a chance that it was an in situ hint: "Wake up! Look around! There's a blaze nearby!" Maybe that was the purpose of the verse "Look quickly down"—to point to this tree. Only a searcher would understand its meaning. A change of plans was in order; I would have to extend my stay.

Forrest said that there wasn't a human trail, "in very close proximity" to where he hid the treasure. Even though the memorial plaque and the false blaze were, by my definition, "in very close proximity" to a human trail, I extended my trip by three full days to meticulously search a few hundred feet in each direction surrounding both. The only things I found were nails, soda cans, and bottle caps. I didn't even find an old Wheat Penny for my trouble. As payment for going off-trail, I took the trash out with me. And, for the curious, I left the false blaze as I found it.

All of these blazes had my treasure-hunting senses tingling. I wanted to continue searching near them, but I had already extended my trip longer than I had anticipated. I still needed to explore the rest of the area between the trailhead and the lake before I headed home, so I reluctantly moved on.

Forrest said that the place where he hid the treasure chest was safe. Elsewhere in this book, I discuss the meaning of the word "safe." My opinion aligns with Forrest's. The area is safe—if you stay on the trail, hike in the summer months, and do not do anything stupid. If you do what I did, the subjectiveness of the word "safe" comes into play. There are moss-covered rocks in the area camouflaged by fallen leaves and branches that are deceptively slippery. More slippery than the moss-covered rocks are the wet rocks near the creek. If you get too close, you *will* slip and fall in. And if you fall in, there is a good chance you will not be climbing back out.

Do not risk your life searching for something that was never there. I searched that area to be thorough and because the whole purpose of that first trip was reconnaissance. I didn't have an explanation for the rest of the poem at that time. I did six months later.

Pursuing It With Eager Feet

I SPENT eight or nine days total in the general area surrounding Mystic Lake in 2019, exploring anything that caught my eye on the three-mile hike to the lake. With a water filter and an endless water supply from the creek and lake, staying out all day was not a problem.

One of the first things I noticed was all the nooks and crannies. They were everywhere. Forrest could have hidden a thousand chests in the area, and no one would stumble across any of them.

About a mile up from the trailhead, after crossing the creek, there is a section of the forest where many trees have names and messages carved into them. Some carvings are decades old. Most are from school kids proclaiming their fondness for one another. I considered the possibility of another treasure-related message in the carvings but didn't look extensively that trip. I glanced at the carvings but did not have time for a thorough search of every tree. There were a *lot* of messages.

If you walk that trail from mid-July through August, be on the lookout for the deep purple of ripe huckleberries. They are especially abundant after you cross over the creek. Huckleberries are the undisputed king of berries. They're kind of like blueberries but with flavor. I've heard tell that bears are fond of huckleberries, so be on the lookout for them as well. The occasional wild raspberry, strawberry, or thimbleberry may also make an appearance. There are also a few berries that I would be less than enthusiastic about eating —including one that, unfortunately, looks a lot like a huckleberry.

There was still a bit of snow and ice on the trail on my trip in early June of 2019. If you are not used to hiking over snow and ice, wait until summer is in full bloom before heading out. Although it was June, a chill was in the air, and the threatening clouds reminded me that this was part of the Rocky Mountains, where one should expect any weather at any time.

From the trailhead to the pass overlooking Mystic Lake, the trail rises about 1,300 feet. The lake's far shore is three miles away and can barely be made out by the naked eye. One and a half miles from the trailhead, the trees thin out, and the path transitions into areas with rock tailings and boulders. Hiking up the switchbacks in this section is where the majority of the vertical climb occurs. A mountain goat would do well here.

The trail winds down the other side of the pass and continues along Mystic Lake's south shore. A half-mile after reaching the shore, the Mystic Lake Trail (trail #19) intersects the Phantom Creek Trail (trail #17). The Phantom Creek Trail heads south from the intersection and then up and over Froze-to-Death Plateau. Yes, a possible connection between Froze-to-Death Plateau and the poem verse "Your effort will be worth the cold" occurred to me. Of course, it did.

My 2019 trip ended near the intersection of Trail #19 and Trail #17. I walked up the Phantom Creek Trail for several hundred feet and explored some nooks, a few crannies, and a couple of large group campsites. You couldn't ask for a better place to set up camp and stay for a few days. Note that there are no facilities there—it's just an open area under the trees. Note also that camping in the middle of a forest is different from camping in a campground. If you ever decide to camp in the woods, pay special attention to what every book on the subject says about bears and food and how not to become an unfortunate statistic.

Phantom Creek Trail sign at the intersection of trails #19 and #17

I did not expect to find the chest during that first trip in 2019; that was a reconnaissance expedition. With so many potential treasure-hiding locations and with so many blazes, I had my work cut out for me. If I were ever going to find the treasure chest, the poem would have to direct me the rest of the way.

My focus shifted back to reading books, deconstructing sentences, and studying maps. There were missing pieces, and I couldn't move forward without finding them.

The Place Where a Story Ended

THE MOST PROMISING leads I found during my boots-on-the-ground trip to Mystic Lake were the four blazes. I dove right back into research mode as soon as I got home.

Nine months earlier, having just started researching in earnest, my reaction was to set the books down and back away. I sensed that Forrest had a deep and personal attachment to the location and was not sure whether I wanted to continue. Two weeks after I returned from my trip, that feeling resurfaced.

The memorial plaque to the young Boy Scout, Mark Edward Von Seggern, is the blaze. After making three crucial connections, there was no doubt in my mind. The blaze—*that blaze*—is the heart of the poem, both in position and in meaning. This is where the poem reaches a turning point. This is the place where a story ended.

On May 20, 1979, Boy Scout Troop 416, out of Columbus, Montana, was hiking from the Mystic Lake Trailhead to Mystic Lake, where they planned to spend the day fishing. There was still a lot of snow on the trail, especially at the top of the pass. 12-year-old Mark Edward Von Seggern was hiking just behind scoutmaster Ron Braley when Braley heard a scream and turned. Von Seggern had slipped on the snow and slid for about 50 feet before he fell off the edge and plunged another 150 feet. He was dead by the time the scoutmaster and another man were able to reach him. The other individual was only identified as "another hiker."

> "Braley's dog, a golden retriever, named Chief, ran after the boy, trying to save him, but the dog fell off the edge and was killed too...Braley and another man climbed down to the boy and found his body and the dog's body within five feet of each other."
>
> *Billings Gazette* – May 22, 1979

Two helicopters were called to the scene but were unable to land due to the challenging terrain. The helicopters hovered overhead as they recovered the body.

Another turning point in the poem occurs here as the poem's encoding morphs, such that synonyms and homophones play a more prominent role. "If you've been wise...and found the blaze." The phrase "Be prepared" is synonymous with "be wise." Having a blaze occur right where I was looking for one and having synonyms for both "blaze" and "been wise" forged into that physical blaze might be a coincidence, but it is the type of coincidence that deserves a great deal of investigation. In case it was not clear, the term "mark" is synonymous with "blaze." "If you've been wise and found Mark."

I understand if you are skeptical; I was skeptical too, at first. All of my doubts vanished after making a few critical connections.

Some might point out Forrest's claim that the location was safe. Although there may be disagreement over whether Forrest meant that the chest's hiding place was safe versus the roads, trails, and waterways leading to that location, this was clearly not safe for the young boy who lost his life.

While the term "safe" is both subjective and relative, I have hiked that trail many times and, in my opinion, it is "safe"—keeping in mind that "safe" does not mean that there is no possibility of harm. I've encountered a variety of hikers on the trail, including elderly couples in their 70s, families with young children and pets, and even a mother with a baby in a front-facing carrier. They, too, presumably, believed it was a safe hike. However, accidents can happen anywhere, and this trail is no exception. The undersheriff at the time agreed:

> "The undersheriff said the spot in the trail where the accident occurred was "a real bad section of the trail," but not really treacherous. He said the boy's death was an unusual accident."
>
> Billings Gazette – May 22, 1979

The Catcher in the Rye

IN THE "IMPORTANT LITERATURE" chapter of *The Thrill of the Chase*, Forrest tells a story about reading J.D. Salinger's *The Catcher in the Rye*. The entirety of "Important Literature" is full of hints, but *The Catcher in the Rye* was unique; it was the only book that Forrest did not throw in the trash. Well, he did throw it in the trash, but he fished it back out again.

Forrest said he felt that *The Catcher in the Rye* was about him; it was his very own storyline. Forrest said his self-confidence was shot and that he would still be down if JD had not insinuated that Forrest write his autobiography—or add on to JD's story. I mention this because that is one of the reasons I decided to write this book; Forrest insinuated that I should finish the story—or add on to it.

You cannot read *The Catcher in the Rye* and come out the other end without thinking that it may hold a hint or two. There was the Navajo blanket purchased in Yellowstone Park, a quote about the difference between "partly true" and "all true," a visit to the Museum of Natural History, and puddles of water with gasoline rainbows. All of those called back to *The Thrill of the Chase*.

One part of *The Catcher in the Rye* that did not stand out to me when I read it was Chapter 22, near the end of the book. It was not until after obtaining the Billings Gazette article about young Mark Edward Von Seggern's accident that the Chapter 22 connection became apparent:

"I keep picturing all these little kids playing some game in this big field of rye and all. Thousands of little kids and nobody's around—nobody big, I mean—except me. And I'm standing on the edge of some crazy cliff. What I have to do, I have to catch everybody if they start to go over the cliff—I mean, if they're running and they don't look where they're going, I have to come out from somewhere and catch them. That's all I'd do all day. I'd just be the catcher in the rye and all. I know it's crazy, but that's the only thing I'd really like to be."

J.D. Salinger— *The Catcher in the Rye*

Tarry Scant with Marvel Gaze

THE BLAZE in the poem represents a crucial turning point. One key reason is that it is at this point where the understanding of words, their synonyms, and homophones take on a pivotal role.

In the poem verse, "But tarry scant with marvel gaze," "tarry scant" could mean "don't dawdle" or it could mean "stay a little while" (scant is synonymous with "several"). How's that for making a poem challenging to decipher? "Marvel gaze" brings up thoughts of *The Wizard of Oz*, *Marvel Comics*, spyglasses, and wonderment. "Tarry scant with marvel gaze" is a perplexing verse at first glance.

In most of Forrest's interviews, he emphasized looking up the meanings of words, making sure he had the correct definitions of the words he used. Since words can have multiple definitions, what is the "correct" definition of a word? It's the definition that fits the meaning the author had in mind. If the "correct definition" is a definition that I've never heard, I will not understand what is said. To fully understand Forrest's words, it is necessary to use the same definitions that Forrest used.

That seems reasonable, but how is it possible to know what definitions Forrest used? Keep in mind that I was trying to pull out hidden meanings for words in a game. I was not analyzing everyday conversation; I was analyzing sentences that Forrest had painstakingly put together and whose purpose was to hide a clue or a hint. The primary method I used for this was to deconstruct a sentence into its components, create a list of possibilities for each component, and then reconstruct the sentence using different combinations of possibilities that made syntactic sense. Another thing to keep in mind is that I was using Forrest's Fennglish rules—which meant the rules were as flexible as Forrest needed them to be.

When discussing the definitions of words in interviews, Forrest liked to use the word "several" as an example and ask whether the interviewer or the audience knew what "several" meant. Forrest would then dismiss the answer, correct or not, and come back with his favorite definition of that word: "More than two, but not many." Why was Forrest so stuck on that particular definition? Was he trying to emphasize that the definition you choose determines the meaning of what is written and how it's read?

Because Forrest was hitting his audience over the head with the idea of looking up the meanings of words, looking up the meanings of words was near the top of my to-do list. This really hit home with the verse, "But tarry scant with marvel gaze." Taking "tarry scant with marvel gaze" and reversing the order yields, "gaze marvel with scant tarry." Taking those five words and substituting synonyms result in "witness accident on narrow trail." This sealed the blaze in my mind and caused me to reflect on what had happened on that trail over forty years ago.

If you are having trouble with the idea of reversing the order of words, note that it was a common theme in Forrest's writings. Forrest often talked about reflections, mirrors, and the reversal of information. I've given several examples in earlier chapters. And Forrest included too many numerical palindromes to be a coincidence. Forrest even talked about riding backward bicycles. As Forrest's "mirror writing" was so conspicuous, looking backward, as well as forward, was built into my methodology from the start.

Indulgence

WHEN I FIRST STARTED SEARCHING FOR the treasure chest, I watched every interview with Forrest I could find. Wandering into the comments section of a few of those first videos was like Mr. Toad's Wild Ride at Disneyland. The comments section of most of the Internet is like that, so it was not a surprise. Anyway, I did not stay long.

One thing that puzzled me was that a few people were using the word "indulgence" in a way that didn't make sense. "Indulgence was never in Yellowstone," someone would say. What the heck did *that* mean? "What a bunch of nuts," I thought. I later found out the meaning of their words.

Forrest had given the treasure chest the name "Indulgence." Forrest said he had initially named the chest "Tarzan" but had later changed it to "Indulgence." Tarzan? Indulgence? Why did he give the chest a name at all? Why those names? Tarzan? I was not sure what to make of Forrest's naming conventions; this information just meant that I now had more potential hints to decode.

The most common definition of indulgence is related to self-indulgence. Forrest Fenn, the eccentric millionaire and former art dealer, had hidden a treasure chest full of gold and jewels, written a poem and a book about the treasure, and then dared people to find it. I was not sure about "Tarzan," but that definition of "Indulgence" sounded about right.

For the solution I am presenting here, other definitions of indulgence are more applicable, including: apology, absolution, redemption, and atonement. Was Forrest the other hiker who witnessed the boy's accident? Did Forrest think he could have reacted quicker and therefore felt partly to blame? Did the rescue of the young boy bring back buried memories? Was this about something more?

Forrest said that the location was a "very special place" to him, and that he had an "almost umbilical" connection to the site—a bond so strong he wanted to die there. I wondered briefly if Forrest meant that in the past tense.

For searchers, the poem was about finding a chest full of gold and jewels. For Forrest, the poem was about this special place. The chest was a lure to get someone to the location and to figure out the story. "Indulgence" was starting to make sense.

Deep-Thinking Searcher Bonus

"The Unfortunate Hiccup" in Forrest's third memoir, *Once Upon a While*, is not about golf, and the word "libation" is not about alcohol.

Method in the Madness

I WAS confident that I had found it—the memorial plaque was the blaze. And now I felt as if I was hovering near the true purpose for the chase and why the location was so special to Forrest. But there was a problem. Forrest's statements surrounding the blaze and the last clue were a tangled mess of contradictions.

The fourth stanza of the poem reads:

> *If you've been wise and found the blaze,*
> *Look quickly down, your quest to cease,*
> *But tarry scant with marvel gaze,*
> *Just take the chest and go in peace.*

That looked unambiguous on the surface: "Find the blaze; look down; you're done; don't hang around; take the chest; go in peace." This interpretation appeared to be reinforced by two statements from Forrest:

1. When asked how far the chest was from the blaze, Forrest replied, "I did not take the measurement, but logic tells me that if you don't know where the blaze is, it

really doesn't matter. If you can find the blaze, though, the answer to your question will be obvious."
2. "When you get to the last clue, look down because that's where the treasure chest is."

The problem was that if the memorial plaque was the blaze, and if the blaze was the last clue, then the two statements above conflicted with another comment made by Forrest, "There isn't a human trail in very close proximity to where I hid the treasure." This was a problem because the plaque was right on top of the trail, and there was no treasure chest in sight. The water pipe across the side of the mountain, however, was nowhere near a human trail. I wonder if anybody ever searched up there?

The memorial plaque was the blaze of the fourth stanza; I was sure of it. The area surrounding Mystic Lake fit too well, and everything else lined up perfectly. In the chapter titled "Pioneers of a Different Sort," I predicted that a blaze would be east of Mystic Lake's west end and west of the Mystic Lake Trailhead. And there, right where it was supposed to be, was not just a blaze, but the perfect blaze. It had to be correct.

There was another problem. According to my count, the blaze was not the last clue but clue #5, smack dab in the middle of the poem. For the blaze to be the last clue, every line of the poem from "Begin it where warm waters halt" to "If you've been wise and found the blaze" would have to hold a clue, and, according to my methodology's definition of "clue," that was not possible. Did it matter? If I was standing in front of the blaze, who cares if the count was off?

Specific interpretations of Forrest's words implied that the chest was close to the blaze; that is true. But Forrest said a lot of stuff. Cherry-picking a selection of Forrest's quotes and marrying them to interpretations that fit a particular line of reasoning might not have the best outcome.

Another thing that Forrest said was that it was risky to discount any word in the poem; all of the words were important. Well, I just disregarded half the words in the poem and still found the blaze.

What I did not do—at that time—was solve the poem. However you look at it, if "Begin it where warm waters halt" is the first clue, and "If you've been wise and found the blaze" is the last clue, and you can get from the first to the last without the other stanzas of the poem, and the chest was right by the blaze, then half the poem is unnecessary.

The idea of discounting half the poem, combined with my method insisting that the blaze was clue #5 and not clue #9, was harshing my mellow.

I was missing something important, so I did what I had done previously when confronted by too much conflicting information. I gave control of the situation back to my methodology. My methodology dismissed all potential hints and herrings as noise. As far as it was concerned, Forrest's conflicting statements did not exist. If "tarry scant with marvel gaze" had a deeper meaning, the surrounding verses could have deeper meanings as well. And if I was right about the blaze and tarry scant, I was confident that any conflicting statements would no longer be conflicting by the time I reached the last clue.

Navigational Nuptials

"THE PERSON who finds the treasure will have studied the poem over and over, and thought, and analyzed and moved with confidence. Nothing about it will be accidental," Forrest insisted. The only thing was, I could move with confidence to the blaze, but no further. There were too many places to hide a chest between the trailhead and the lake. Walking with confidence past the blaze was not possible without more information. The key had to be in the second half of the poem.

I could, of course, have been wrong. Maybe the blaze I had found wasn't *the* blaze. Maybe the false blaze wasn't false. Maybe I wasn't even in the correct state. Maybe the method led me down a false path. Maybe, but I did not think so. All the evidence said otherwise. The method was not only working, it was working scarily well and making accurate predictions. The method got me to the blaze—it wouldn't be wise to abandon it now.

According to my methodology, the next step was to use the memorial plaque as the new starting point. From there, the challenge was to marry the remaining verses of the poem with specific locations on a map, treating each verse as a potential clue. Research into the area surrounding Mystic Lake identified several nearby suitors, each with its own unique characteristics:

- *Tarry Scant with Marvel Gaze:* That verse not only confirmed the blaze but also pointed to a specific location up the trail, roughly near the top of the pass.
- *19/17:* Forrest said that a couple of people had been within 200 feet of the treasure, and many people had been within 500 feet. Many people hike trail #19 and a few hike trail #17. That screamed of the possibility of a 500-foot by 400-foot search area heading up trail #17.
- *East Rosebud Lake:* If you hike backward on trail #17 from trail #19, you will reach the Phantom Creek Trailhead discussed in the chapter, "I Learned the Truth at Seventeen." Did the path in the poem lead in that direction? Half a mile south of the Phantom Creek Trailhead is East Rosebud Lake—a shape I recognized immediately. On page 133 of *The Thrill of the Chase*, Forrest said, "I dreamed the other night that I had been reincarnated as Captain Kidd and went to Gardiners Island looking for the treasure." Although Gardiners Island is made of earth and the lake is water, the shapes are remarkably similar. Was it a coincidence? Was it a pointer to East Rosebud Lake? *Note: The tiny hamlet of Alpine surrounds the shore of East Rosebud Lake. Alpine is a small and private community. If you don't have an invitation, you should veer east around the lake and head to the East Rosebud campground or trailhead.*
- *Wyoming:* The first line of the fifth stanza in the poem is, "So why is it that I must go..." Could "why'" be a play on words, hinting at WY for Wyoming? A hikeable trail does lead from the blaze to Wyoming. In a straight line, the Wyoming border is about 16.5 miles from the blaze. It's a somewhat longer hike. The bottleneck between the second and third clues was the distance. Could that be a factor here as well?

Except for the "tarry scant with marvel gaze" location, all of these possibilities had one thing in common: none of them were marriage material.

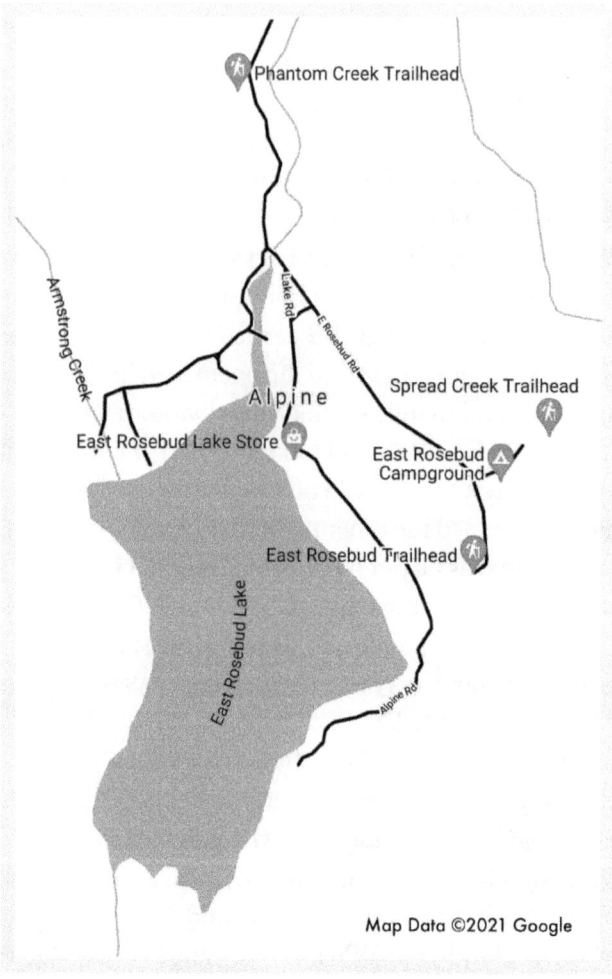

East Rosebud Lake & Surrounding Area

Navigational Nuptials

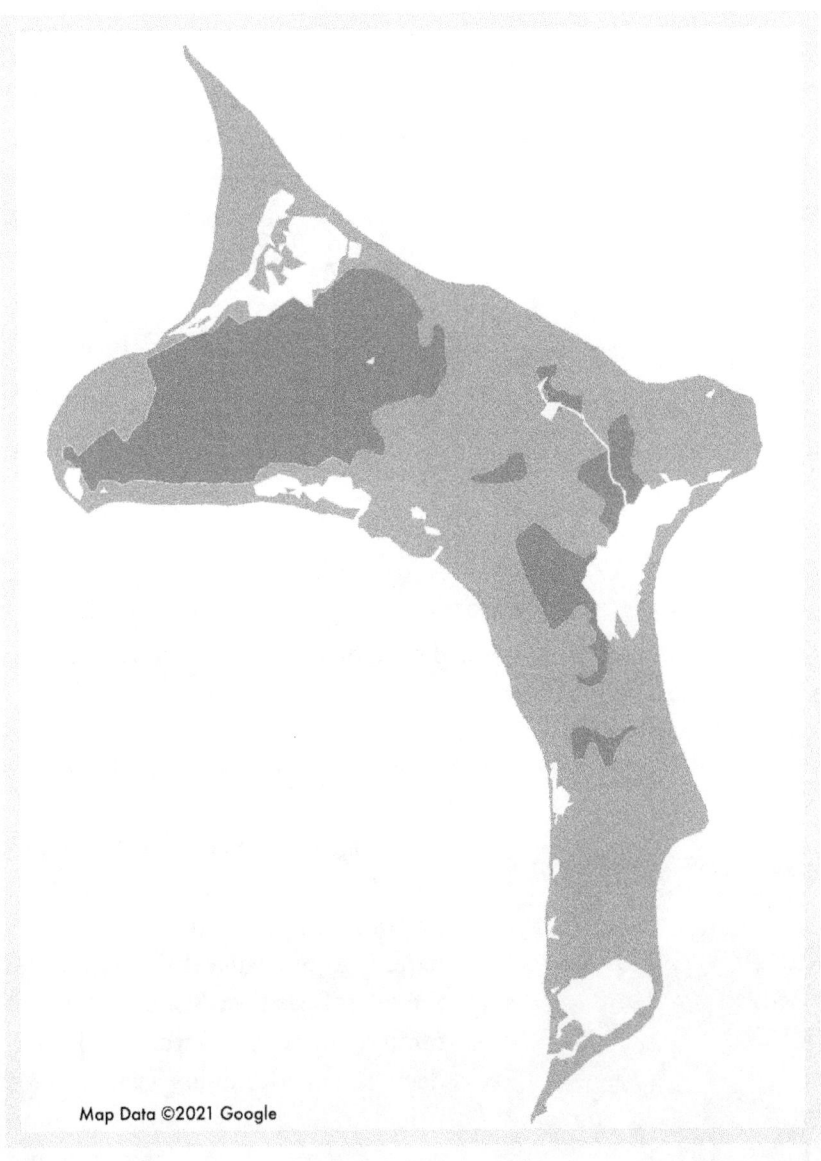

Gardiners Island

The Big Picture

FINDING similarities between the shape of East Rosebud Lake and Gardiners Island shook loose a particular filter in my mind. Once I made the connection, the filter was impossible to turn off. Like those hidden 3D stereograms, once you see one, it's easier to see others.

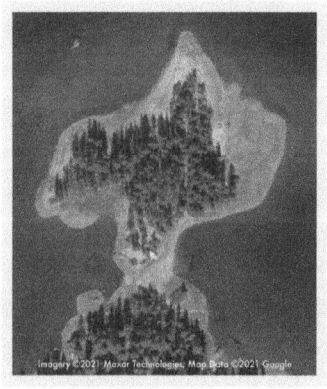

I had seen that same Gardiners Island shape somewhere else. Near the tail end of Mystic Lake, shown here, is a peninsula that juts up into the lake. Like East Rosebud Lake, it reminded me of Gardiners Island. Seeing that Gardiners Island shape twice in such close proximity indicated a type of bias that did not boost my confidence. But still, I could not help but wonder if Forrest was hinting at this peninsula.

The shape of Gardiners Island was intriguing, but looking at the big picture was more so. Forrest's continued emphasis on "looking at the big picture" and saying that a child may have an advantage converged as I zoomed out from the "Gardiners Island peninsula" of Mystic Lake and watched a story reveal itself.

Just to the west of Mystic Lake, connected by West Rosebud Creek, is Island Lake. The two lakes are essentially one larger lake with a narrow slip of land parting the waters and West Rosebud Creek flowing between them. Viewing Mystic Lake and Island Lake together in the same frame, I saw Beowulf chasing Bip. It brought a smile to my face, but like the nearby Gardiners Island shapes, it had to be a coincidence.

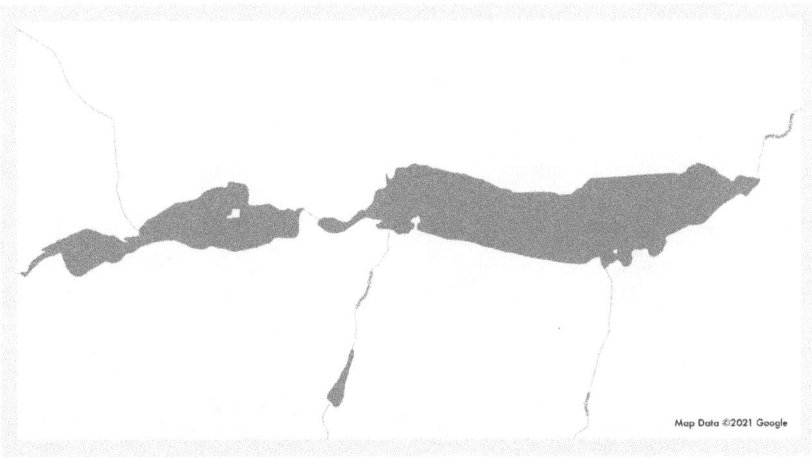

Island Lake and Mystic Lake — Beowulf Chasing Bip

For those who do not know, Beowulf was Forrest's pet alligator, and Bip was Forrest's beloved little dachshund. In Scrapbook 227, Forrest recalled that, after selling his art gallery, when the new gallery owner was showing her insurance agent around the property, they saw Beowulf chasing a small dog across the yard. When the new owner then received a higher than expected insurance quote, Beowulf had to find a new home.

Forrest had shared that story a few times before. In the previous tellings, Beowulf was chasing a duck, not a dog. In Scrapbook 227, which came out in November 2019, Forrest changed the duck to a small dog. He didn't specify whether or not the dog was Bip.

I wasn't trying to link anything to the poem at that moment; I was relaxing and having a bit of fun. Some of the research, such as looking up definitions for every word in the poem and books, was tedious, and I took an occasional break to clear my mind.

The image of Beowulf chasing Bip was a coincidence, I knew it was a coincidence. But confirmation bias was tempting me, whispering in my ear, "Every other time you saw something that made you smile, it was *not* a coincidence. What other coincidences are lurking nearby?"

The Thrill of the Chase

WHEN I PANNED over to Island Lake and zoomed in on Beowulf's silhouette, something immediately stood out: the eye of the alligator. It bears a striking resemblance to a boot or a shoe—and could that be Elton John's "Crocodile Rock?" Long-time searchers will recall Forrest's numerous stories about losing one or both shoes. In a 2017 interview with Dal Neitzel, Forrest remarked, "I don't know why I get myself in terrible situations [where] I don't have any shoes on."

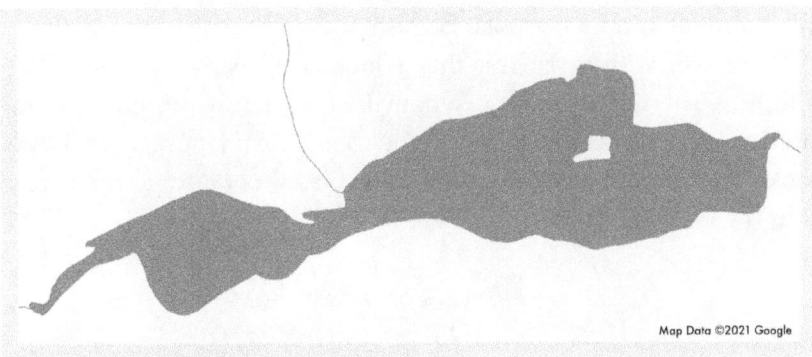

Island Lake

The topic of shoes often appeared in Forrest's tales, and not just in those instances where he found himself without them. There were stories about his favorite hush puppies, house shoes named "Cuddles," shoes made from old truck tires, horseshoes, logging shoes, and more. There were big shoes in Scrapbook 212 and a shoe store two blocks away from the bank in Scrapbook 215. Forrest even threatened to make shoes out of Beowulf if Beowulf ever lunged at him.

In the Moby Dickens talk Forrest gave in 2013, he said, "I knew where I wanted to hide the treasure chest, so it was easy for me to put one foot down and then step on it to get to the next foot." That is peculiar phrasing, but I could accept it.

In 2015, during the Richard Eeds Show, Richard asked Forrest, "What kind of shoes? What kind of footprints did you leave? What kind of boots did you have on?" Forrest replied, "Well if I told you that, you'd go out and find it." What's odd about this exchange is that the question is so out of place. Listen to the interview or read the transcript, and you will see how well it doesn't flow. Interviewees have been known to suggest questions for interviewers to ask.

I took a break to look at a boot on the map, as I could only research so many word definitions before my mind would start working against me. I was not just looking for the definitions of the words in the poem but for the meanings of every word that Forrest had said concerning the chase. I suspected that Forrest spoke Fennglish more often than he spoke English.

Five words from Forrest that I looked up early on were "The Thrill of the Chase." Using synonyms for each word, one translation of that is, "The Blaze of the Boot." And now, here I was looking at a giant boot. Confirmation bias was taunting me again. Was the booty on that boot?

Deep-Thinking Searcher Bonus

The total area of "Booty Island" in Island Lake is just over 2 acres. Recall that Forrest said that his "allotment of public acreage" was "exactly 2.086 acres." Did Forrest hide something under a rock in the cooling waters somewhere in his allotted public acreage?

Deep-Thinking Searcher Double Bonus

In *The Thrill of the Chase,* Forrest described the magical clearing above the waterfall in Vietnam as "about 300 feet across." Forrest only gave the one dimension. Assuming 300-foot by 300-foot square, that would be 90,000 square feet or 2.066 acres.

Deep-Thinking Searcher Triple Bonus

Rotated 90 degrees counter-clockwise, the shape of Booty Island looks like a short-handled axe. In the *Too Far to Walk* chapter "Treasures Galore," Forrest gives an offhand mention to a "double-bitted axe." There's a curious synonym for "bit" that, combined with "double," might be applicable here.

Booty Island and a Double-Bitted Axe

See if you can figure out what the figure looks like as it is rotated in other directions.

Bullseye

BOOTY ISLAND WAS MESMERIZING and dots were connecting faster than I could keep track. I zoomed in and switched to satellite view. It still looked *boot-ish*, but with more pronounced toe and heel sections.

And then, although I was viewing it upside down, I saw something else. I saw Bessie, the cow that Forrest's family owned when Forrest was a boy. Or was it Cody, the buffalo Forrest tried capturing years ago, seven miles west of the town of West Yellowstone? Rotated 180 degrees, the boot had become a stump-tailed cow.

A possibly relevant quote from the dust jacket of The *Thrill of the Chase* came to mind: "It takes...enough confidence in a maverick to know that the treasure is really there for the taking." Forrest referred to himself as a maverick off and on, the implied meaning being an independent-minded person.

Another well-known definition of the word maverick is an unbranded calf or cow. That definition made more sense in this context. "It takes...enough confidence in a maverick to know that the treasure is really there for the taking." This maverick was seven miles west of the trailhead parking lot—one would have to have absolute confidence in it before making that trek.

"The Maverick" — Cody on Island Lake

There are three trees right where the eye would be on the maverick's head—a "bull's eye." A year earlier, I had made a note about a possible definition for the phrase "in the wood" from the poem verse, "If you are brave and in the wood." "In the wood" is a dart term meaning the dart has found the bullseye of the target. An eye in an eye? Did Beowulf and Bessie have their eyes on the prize?

Either confirmation bias was being exceptionally cruel to me, or I was looking at the resting place of Forrest's treasure chest, Indulgence. Was that it? Was I looking at the end of the poem?

The poem's connection from the first clue through the blaze was solid, earning a perfect Interpretation Score. If I could connect the dots between the blaze and the bullseye, I would have a complete solution to the poem. And if that solution were correct, that would mean that Forrest's poem followed a course for over 200 miles down a river and then up a creek before coming to rest at a precise spot on an island in an impossibly small section of the Rocky Mountains.

I considered the odds of discovering another solution of comparable quality elsewhere in the Rocky Mountains. I thought the chances of that to be somewhere between slim and none.

Deep-Thinking Searcher Bonus

Forrest's second memoir, *Too Far to Walk*, contains a half-dozen or so subchapters, or chapters between chapters, each adding a bit of flavor to the memoir. The subchapter on page 89 is titled "bullseye."

Deep-Thinking Searcher Double Bonus

In "My War For Me," Forrest talked about flying down the Eastern Seaboard. While passing over Philadelphia, Forrest closed his left fist, stuck his thumb out, moved it an inch from his left eye, and exclaimed that he had "covered up millions" with his thumb. Rotated 90 degrees clockwise, the shape of Booty Island looks like a left fist with the thumb sticking out. The tip of that thumb is right over the top of the bullseye.

The "Thumb"

Order from Chaos

"MAVERICK...CODY...BULLSEYE...THAT'S IT!" Those were my first thoughts upon seeing the image. In my gut, I knew that was where Indulgence lay, but nothing I saw while looking at "the big picture" meant a thing if I could not get the poem to take me there. My method was indifferent to everything outside the poem—information outside the poem could neither add to nor subtract from the Interpretation Score of a solution. It would argue with Forrest himself if he were to contradict the poem.

My method ignored Beowulf, Bip, and the boot. It was uninterested in Forrest's "Don't make the alligator mad until you've crossed the river" statement and how you might have to do just that to get to the bullseye. It was unmoved by the fact that the elevation of the island was halfway between Forrest's two elevation extremes of 5,000 feet and 10,200 feet. It was impervious to suggestions that Olga's 3-foot long bathtub might be hinting at the 3-mile long "bathtub" of Mystic Lake. It was indifferent to the fact that there is a one-room schoolhouse in Columbus, Montana that happens to be about 50 miles down a (partially) dirt road to the bullseye.

My method did not care about Forrest's allusions to islands. It didn't care about Forrest's signature with an odd dot in the loop of the second F. It didn't care that Forrest twice alluded to finding a treasure on an island. It didn't care that the quote "clouds had mountains in them" from Scrapbook 223 could be referring to an island. It didn't care that Island Lake is really just an overly broad and deep section of West Rosebud Creek or how that might relate to the Rosetta Stone, a recurring anecdote that Forrest told.

My method did not care about Forrest's veiled references to eyes. It didn't care that "Eisenhower" could be interpreted as "Eyes in Howe(r)." It didn't care that "Einstein"—Forrest liked to quote Einstein—could be interpreted as "Eye in Stein." It didn't care that Scrapbook 227 had to do with alligator shoes and eyes or that Scrapbook 228 had to do with shoes and eyes or that Scrapbook 229 associated the number 8 with a "shoe buckle" and the number 9 with an "eye bead."

My method did not care that Forrest's statement, "Only a few are in tight focus with a word that is key" could be reformatted to read, "Only a few are in tight focus with a word. That is: key." It didn't care that "tight focus" had to do with eyes or that the "word that is key" was "key," which is another term for island.

My method did not care about any of the hints mentioned earlier. Nor did it care how many hints produced lines that cross within walking distance of Island Lake. My method didn't even care that the latitude of the Hidden Treasure mine passed right through the middle of Booty Island.

And my method did not care that Scrapbook 214 mentions a small blaze at the halfway mark.

Neither did my method care about anything external to the poem that would subtract from a solution. It didn't care about the distance between the parking lot and the island. It didn't care about Forrest's suggestion that if you have a search partner, best have them wait in the car. It didn't care about Forrest's statement that Google Earth cannot help with the last clue.

My method just wanted to marry lines in the poem to locations on a map. One thing my method liked quite a lot was the bullseye. The bullseye was marriage material, but only if the poem led there.

A one-room schoolhouse in Columbus, Montana, 48.5 miles from the bullseye. "My father always drove about 50 miles out of our way, down a little dirt road to a one-room schoolhouse."

The picture above shows Forrest's signature with the ever-present dot in the middle of the second F. My proofreader thought I should include these pictures—my method was indifferent toward them.

The Bip Theory

IN THE EFFORT TO leave no hint unexamined, I would sometimes stare at Beowulf chasing Bip while thinking abstract thoughts. One day, as my thoughts wandered close to the edge of reason, a big grin crossed my face.

Looking at Google Maps (map view, not satellite view), I was eyeing Huckleberry Creek as it flowed into the tail end of Mystic Lake. Following the creek up the canyon, the first small lake is Huckleberry Lake, just below Princess Lake.

Given that Beowulf is chasing Bip in this scene, it is not unreasonable to imagine Bip being frightened and, perhaps, losing bladder control and depositing a puddle somewhere out in the woods. With this in mind and a starting point at Huckleberry Lake, I saw an alternative interpretation for the poem.

Beginning at Huckleberry Lake as "where warm waters halt," aka "Bip's Drip," I saw a canyon down, a home of brown (where warm waters start), a "no place for the meek" between Beowulf and Bip, "nigh" meaning "turn left," cold water, the blaze of the boot, and the same "in the wood" bullseye. A silhouette of this scene is shown below.

No, this was not part of my solution. It's just what happens when I've been awake for too long. I still can't help seeing it whenever I look at that section of a map. I wonder if Forrest saw it?

Speaking of Bip, I should mention Scrapbook 243, "I Remember Bip." Released in November 2019, Forrest's reminisces about his friend of seventeen years. The scrapbook includes images from Bip's autobiography titled *BIP*, which Eric Sloane illustrated. Some of the illustrations in the scrapbook might give one a better feel for the connection between the silhouette of Mystic Lake and Bip.

"I Remember Bip" is an entertaining and touching story. Since I had already found the bullseye by the time I read it, the hints contained in the story were easy to spot.

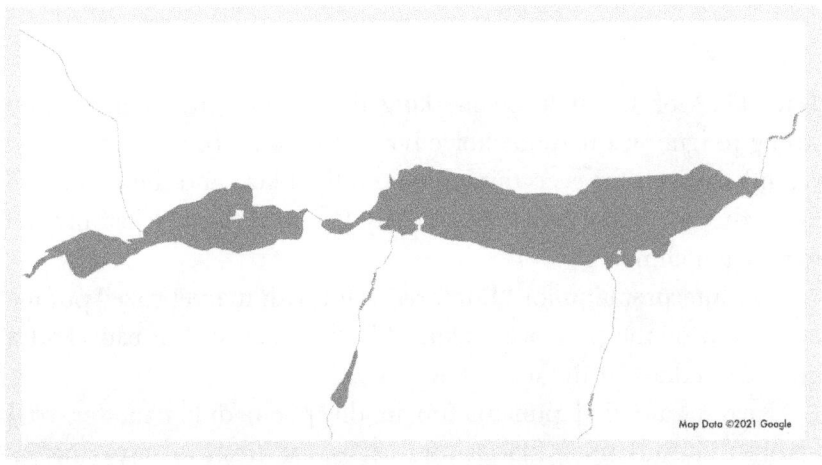

Island Lake and Mystic Lake — Beowulf Chasing Bip

A Sound Solution

THE IDEA of the bullseye marking the poem's endpoint was too strong to ignore; I had no choice but to follow it. To do so, I needed to find a match for everything between the blaze and the bullseye. I knew the two endpoints and what lay between them. I just needed to play matchmaker.

My interpretation for "But tarry scant with marvel gaze" put me at the top of the pass overlooking Mystic Lake, so I already had a good candidate for the sixth clue.

Forrest said that punctuation in the poem didn't matter, so I ignored it. And since islands and eyes were fresh on my mind, a possibility from the fifth stanza was immediately apparent:

> *So why is it that I must go,*
> *And leave my trove for all **to seek?***
> ***The answer I** already know,*
> *I've done it tired, and now I'm weak.*

Admittedly, the following interpretation might be tinged with a good dose of confirmation bias and seem a bit far-fetched, but I was simply scouting for potential connections. Ignoring punctuation in the poem made the phrase "to seek the answer I" stand out, which I translated as follows:

> Answer » key » island.
> I » eye.

"To seek the answer I" became: *To seek the island eye.* This translation was not a clue, but not everything in the poem is a clue. I had previously documented Forrest's overuse of the word "I" in certain writings and thought that he might be hinting at "eye." One example of this is in *The Thrill of the Chase*, page 45, where Forrest says his father "sold our '36 Chevy and got a '4I Plymouth instead." Look closely at the original text, and you will notice that it is not the number forty-one. Instead, that is the number four, followed by the letter I. Pulling possibilities from previous research gave me more confidence than pulling from elsewhere.

Was this confirmation bias? Yep. But that didn't mean it was wrong; "island eye"—especially at that point in the poem—was a good fit. Besides, I was only playing through the scenario. If the bullseye was not correct, the odds were slim that I would find a good fit for everything else between the blaze and the bullseye.

The next thing that clicked for me was the poem word "trove" in the verse "And leave my trove for all to seek." Looking at my list of possibilities for that word, the synonym "reservoir" popped out. *Reservoir* is a synonym for trove? I would never have guessed. Forrest's advice to look up the meanings of words was paying off.

For those who think I have fallen into a vat of confirmation bias, Forrest spoke explicitly about the word "trove." When talking about the meanings of words in an interview for Playboy magazine, Forrest said, "What's a trove...the word trove is a very important thing. I used the word trove in my poem. Is it [the treasure chest] a trove? Look the word trove up and see how it differs from other words that are similar." Other words that are similar to "trove?" So then, synonyms?

"But tarry scant with marvel gaze" put me at the top of a pass overlooking a reservoir, and the next few lines in the poem were talking about a reservoir? I wasn't going to double-down on that bet, but I also wasn't going to fold. Extending the translation, note that a synonym for the word "leave," as in "and leave my trove for all to seek," is "sail." Defined as a verb, it means "travel through water"—or, in other words, "sail through my reservoir." I was no longer idly entertaining this scenario; it had my full attention.

In retrospect, I was kicking myself for not thinking of this next connection earlier. "So hear me all and listen good" suggested that there might be an audible component to the solution. That was not the part I missed. The part I missed was the thing you would be listening for. Hear what? A sound. Listen for what? A sound. A chapter in *Too Far to Walk* even included the words, "When a sound breaks the calm of the canyon, I know it's something important, and I quickly turn."

To drive the point home hard, two synonyms for "good" are "sound" and "rosy." A rosy sound. A sound on the Rosebud? Hear, listen, good—sound, sound, sound. Every word in the poem was deliberate.

What is a sound? A sound is defined, in one context, as "A relatively narrow passage of water between larger bodies of water or between the mainland and an island." I knew that. I used to live near a sound. This connection came after the fact, which I didn't like, but it fit so perfectly that I decided to look the other way and not tell anybody about my misstep. To make me feel even worse, I just now realized that Gardiners Island is off of Long Island Sound. Dumb, dumb, dumb.

"So hear me all and listen good." A sound. "Your effort will be worth the cold." Cross the cold water of the sound to get to the island—your achievement will be worth it. "If you are brave and in the wood."—Bullseye. Were those wedding bells in the distance?

I was now convinced of the bullseye—filling in the blanks for the rest of the poem was just a formality at this point. Still, that was a long hike, and I would feel better about it with every "t" crossed and every "i" dotted. After a few more days of crossing and dotting, I was looking at a complete solution to the poem.

When I started the chase over a year before, part of me did not think the poem was long enough. It did not look like enough information to lead to a precise spot somewhere in the middle of the Rocky Mountains. If the poem led to such a spot, I thought all the clues had to be close together. That twenty-four seemingly vague lines of a poem spanned over 200 miles and led to such a precise location is still amazing to me.

I had two main qualifiers for any solution. The first qualifier was: does the solution come from just the poem and a map. If the answer to that question was not an unequivocal "YES," then the solution was wrong. The solution might be close, but close is not complete, and this was a pass/fail test. The bullseye solution passed that test effortlessly.

The second qualifier asked FORREST—the Finite Operational Rules to Rate the Estimated Strength of a Theory—what it thought of the solution. FORREST was the method I had designed to judge solutions. FORREST was my impartial jury. FORREST would decide whether I stayed home or went on an adventure. What did FORREST think of the bullseye solution? FORREST told me to pack my bags.

Deep-Thinking Searcher Bonus

I've left out the remaining translations for the benefit of those still seeking the thrill of the chase. The most challenging verse left to translate is probably, "I've done it tired, and now I'm weak." I recommend concentrating on why "done," "tired," and "weak" are all in the same verse. After that, translations for the remaining verses between the blaze and the bullseye should be trivial.

Fly Me to the Moon

ACCORDING TO FORREST, he was 79 or 80 when he made two trips in one afternoon from his vehicle to hide the treasure chest. Forrest admonished people not to go where a 79- or 80-year-old man could not go twice in one afternoon. Forrest does not define "afternoon," but giving him the benefit of the doubt, let's say he means "daylight hours." During summer solstice at the latitude of the bullseye, that would be approximately 16 hours of daylight.

I could make one trip from the trailhead to the bullseye and back easily enough in that timeframe—as long as I wasn't carrying anything. For two trips—28 miles total—I would require a good flashlight. That Forrest, at 80 years old, could do so carrying 25 pounds per trip seemed unlikely.

This is an example of not letting hints or herrings overrule a poem solution. They can guide, but they must conform to the poem, not the other way around. I was not concerned with the distance to the island because I already knew the answer. Forrest's mode of travel to get to the island was not the same one I would be using.

The first line of the poem reads, "As I have gone alone in there." From his first flights in pilot training, Forrest often emphasized being alone while flying. As a combat pilot in Vietnam, Forrest said that he did not want to fly a plane that required two people. Forrest also talked about flying alone down the length of the Eastern Seaboard in "The Philadelphia Caper" portion of "My War for Me." And, of course, there's Forrest's answer to one of the "Six Questions" interviews on *MysteriousWritings.com*: "My favorite flights were those when I headed alone, and at 200 feet, into the teeth of the Rockies, not knowing, or caring, where I would land."

Forrest often told variations of the following story: "I've had eighteen women want to marry me, and my wife asked me today, 'what do you tell these eighteen women when they call you and want to marry you?' I said, well, the first thing I ask them is if they have an airplane." Another time Forrest told this story, the number was 32 women. Sometimes he didn't mention a number. The number varied, but the airplane did not.

During one talk, when Forrest said that he could still go right to the treasure, a woman in the audience asked if he would be willing to take a partner along. Forrest answered, "Do you have an airplane?" She did. Forrest quickly backtracked and said he'd have to think about it.

Then there is the questionable story about Skippy, Forrest's brother, landing a pontoon airplane on Hebgen Lake in Montana. Skippy couldn't take off again because the aircraft did not have enough power for a water takeoff at that altitude. That was back in the 1940s. Airplanes land and take off on lakes at far higher altitudes than that these days.

There is even a hint to this way back at the beginning, on page 15 of *The Thrill of the Chase*: "Now, near the end of my seventy-ninth year, each day tests me in a different way and I know that before too long I'll make my last flight to where even memory itself will never have been."

Not to leave out the reason for the title of this chapter, Forrest was still giving hints about this as late as April 9, 2020. In Scrapbook 252, Forrest talked about a video of a little girl singing, "Fly Me to the Moon." This is reminiscent of page 146 of *The Thrill of the Chase*, where a man is looking up at a bird that has made a nest in a crescent moon—an "island in the sky."

And, of course, there's Forrest's story about flying to the two-acre magical clearing above the waterfall in Vietnam—the place to which he felt so obligated. That's the same trip where Forrest came across the grave markers that affected him so.

Enough stories hinted at Forrest's flying to the treasure's location that the possibility made it into my thoughts early on. That may be why I did not immediately dismiss the bullseye upon noting how far it was from the parking lot—I had always assumed that Forrest had flown to the location.

But just because Forrest flew there didn't mean that I could. I would have to hoof it over seven long miles, find a way across the lake to the island, and then figure out how I would make it back with an additional 42 pounds to carry. I started chanting a mantra, "please let there be a proxy, please let there be a proxy."

Deep-Thinking Searcher Bonus

There are parallels between this situation—Forrest's being able to fly there while searchers have to walk—and Forrest's story about taking his football coach, Concy Wood, on a fishing trip to Grebe Lake in Yellowstone. The finely suited man wearing white sneakers is of particular interest.

Deep-Thinking Searcher Double Bonus

I just double-checked an old note I had made about the meaning of the word "brave" from the poem verse "If you are brave and in the wood." One of the interpretations I wrote down, a synonym for "brave," is "fly in the face of." Fly in the face of the bullseye.

Be Prepared

IT WAS MID-NOVEMBER 2019, when I started planning for a trip to the island. "I would have left that day!" some might exclaim. Maybe, but the area was already snowed in, the days were short, the hike was long, my back complained nonstop, and I did not have the proper equipment. My trip would have to wait until the summer of 2020.

I thought it unlikely that anyone else had the same solution and was sure the treasure was waiting patiently for the clomp of my boots. Feeling confident, I made plans for the first week of July when the snow was melted and the days were long. I had no idea whether the weather would cooperate, but it was more likely to do so in July than November.

For some reason, I felt compelled to send Forrest a coded message telling him of my intentions. Forrest was getting hundreds of emails a day, and the chance he would read mine was slim. The letter was written in Fennglish so that if you didn't know the language, you wouldn't understand. Forrest never replied.

The logistics of getting there and back again were straightforward. I was familiar with the area up to the 19/17 trail intersection, and a topographic map showed the rest of the hike to be mostly level and uncomplicated.

The distance didn't concern me, but my back did. I've had a bad back all my life, and it was already lodging complaints at just the thought of having to carry 50 pounds seven miles. Making multiple trips would help, but the chest itself weighed 22 pounds, and I would have to carry it out whole. That may not sound like a lot, but even an 80-year-old Forrest Fenn could carry more than I could.

I made a compromise with my back. I would purchase a good hunting backpack meant for heavy loads. The pack was designed to transfer weight from the back to the hips, and it worked well. My back was pleased. My hips, on the other hand, noticed the shift in load, and the argument started all over.

My "training" for the excursion consisted of multiple hikes every week. Each hike was between 2 and 14 miles, carrying bags of rice and other kitchen staples in my backpack. Walking wasn't the problem; I could walk all day. The 14-mile round trip to the island would be easy with nothing on my back. I could still make the round trip with a 15-pound backpack, but I would spend the next day in recovery. My upper limit with a 30-pound pack was about 2 miles before my back gave out and I required 2 days of bed rest.

I wasn't sure how, but I was going to make it work no matter what. Secretly, I was counting on adrenaline carrying half the load.

This next part may not make sense, and I am sure some will not believe it. I could have asked someone to go along and help carry the load, but I didn't want to. It had nothing to do with the treasure; it was that I wanted to do it alone. Standing on the eye of the island meant something to me that someone just tagging along could never understand. They would be there for the shiny bits. I would be there to complete a journey, and I didn't want anything getting in the way of that.

The last leg of the journey involved crossing the sound to the island. I had never been there before and did not know what to expect. Satellite images indicated that it might be possible to wade across from the north shore if the water was low enough, but I couldn't count on that. Traveling that far only to find that I couldn't make it the last few hundred feet was not something I was willing to do. I had to be prepared.

I ended up purchasing an Alpaca Packraft. Alpaca makes professional-quality rafts that are meant to be packed into the backcountry. They are light enough to carry but still constructed such that you feel confident that you won't be putting your life in danger. There was no way I was going to put that treasure chest—and me—into a cheap knockoff raft or some cheesy pool toy purchased at the nearest discount superstore.

It was all about being prepared for the unexpected. Were there sharp rocks or sticks in the water that would poke into my boat? I didn't know. I did know that I wanted to err on the side of making it back to the mainland more dry than wet. The finished raft arrived during the third week of May. After a few test floats down a local river, I was more than happy with the purchase.

My training hikes through winter and spring were progressing well, with every outing registering fewer complaints from my back and hips. In a month's time, I would be hitting the road, the finish line within my reach.

As the journey drew nearer, a sense of restlessness washed over me. There were good reasons why the treasure had eluded all seekers so far. But a lingering worry gnawed at me: If I could unravel the mystery, what stopped someone else from doing the same? How likely was it that after ten years of nobody coming close, two searchers had simultaneously found the solution to the poem? No, the chances of that were near zero.

Still, while I kept my distance from the treasure-hunting blogs, I occasionally skimmed the topic titles, looking for a big headline saying that someone had found the treasure. And then, on June 6, 2020, I saw a big headline.

There and Back Again

I ARRIVED at the Emerald Lake Campground on the afternoon of July 1, 2020, and set up camp. The next day, as people were coming to the campground looking for a vacant spot to spend their 4th of July vacation, I was gazing across Island Lake at the bullseye.

The hike to Island Lake was much as I had anticipated, although there were a few surprises. The top of the pass overlooking Mystic Lake was like a wind tunnel that day, threatening to blow me back to the parking lot. Mystic Lake was full to overflowing, and water was cascading 100 feet over the dam's edge to the rocks below, creating a rainbow in the mist. The wind was hardly noticeable once I made it to the trees on the south shore. There were a couple of creek crossings over log "bridges" where careful footing was appropriate and one spot where I lost the trail and had to backtrack, but other than that, the hike was uneventful.

Before I knew it, I broke through the trees and onto the white sandy beach on the eastern shore of Island Lake. The wind, which I had forgotten about, was back with a vengeance—there was no way I would be able to paddle against it to the Island. Maybe if I had a sailboat, I could sail "full and by" up the Rosebud, but I only had a paddle. I would have to hike around and approach from the side.

To the north, West Rosebud Creek was flowing like sand in an hourglass through the strait between Island Lake and Mystic Lake. The scene reminded me of Scrapbook 221. In 1954, Forrest and his wife, Peggy, had rented a house in Mexico Beach, Florida, while Forrest was stationed at Tyndall AFB. Forrest told a story of a beach, two bodies of water with a river flowing between them, and tourists looking to pilfer his seashells. Forrest thought the people picking up his seashells should have asked for permission.

Like so many of Forrest's scrapbooks, this one looked to be full of hints. Forrest described a lake behind his house as going through a cycle of filling until it breached a dam, and then water rushing out until the lake drained into the Gulf of Mexico. This process should be recognizable to anyone familiar with reservoirs like Mystic Lake; reservoirs fill in the spring/summer and drain in the fall/winter.

Ordinarily, there was just a trickle of water between the lake and the gulf in Forrest's tale. But that day, with the lake full, Forrest took a stick and drew a thin line several inches deep to help the water start to flow from the lake. Before long, the usually slow dribble of water had turned into a raging river 40 feet wide and 4 feet deep. Forrest had successfully thwarted the tourists.

West Rosebud Creek is just a trickle of water in the fall and winter as it flows between Island Lake and Mystic Lake. The creek is easy to cross at that time of year. In early July, it was a raging torrent, 40 feet wide and 4 feet deep. I felt like a tourist.

A trail heading north, across the creek, and around Island Lake leads to the shortest crossing from the mainland to the island. While that was the ideal path to the island, I didn't want to risk crossing the 40-foot wide creek at that time of year. Had I been thwarted?

I couldn't go around Island Lake to the north because of the creek, and I couldn't launch from the beach because of the wind. Luckily, there was a third option. There was what looked like a rocky clearing on the lake's south shore across from the island. Although there was no trail leading there, that choice seemed better than the alternatives. I didn't come this far to turn back. I knew before leaving home what I wouldn't find, but I had to finish the journey. I was still going to make it work no matter what.

An hour later, I was launching the packraft and paddling toward the island from that rocky clearing. The wind was working against me, and progress was slow, but just before my arms gave out, I beached the raft on the head of the island—I was standing on the bullseye. *Note to self: make sure you bring enough rope to tie the raft to a tree on windy days, or else be prepared to swim to shore. Alternatively, bring a partner and have him or her wait in the boat.*

The water level in the lake was high enough that the island's "head" was isolated from the "body." The cold water on my tired feet felt fantastic as I walked around the bullseye, exploring.

I stayed on the island for quite a while, lightly exploring and gazing at the surrounding scenery. I never thought the final location had to be a pristine wonderland, but it didn't hurt that it was just that. It will never happen, but I would like to be there during the first snow of winter, with nothing but silence to keep me company.

Getting back to the beach from the island was easy—the wind was eager to see me go.

From the beach on Island Lake, looking at Booty Island in the distance.

The Bullseye

The picture above was taken about one hundred fifty feet from the bullseye. The tide is a little high, and much of the bull's head is underwater, leaving only the bullseye. The moss-covered rocks surrounding the island were as slippery as they looked.

The previous page shows the view from the beach on the eastern shore of Island Lake looking toward the island. The raft I used to row to the island is in the foreground. If it hadn't been for the horseflies, I could have napped all afternoon on that beach.

I took these pictures on July 19, 2021. Thankfully, the wind was calm that day, unlike in 2020, and I could launch from the beach instead of walking around the side of Island Lake. After walking six miles with a heavy pack, the prospect of paddling instead of walking was welcome. Being able to take my shoes off and wade into the lake was a bonus.

From the island looking back at the beach

⚠ BE PREPARED — NEW TRAIL CONDITIONS ⚠

Since my last visit to Island Lake, the landscape has undergone significant changes due to severe flooding in 2022. Many trees have fallen across the path to the lake. This has lead to continual detours for hikers. More notably, the bridge spanning Huckleberry Creek, situated at the western end of Mystic Lake, has been swept away. That was a *very* robust bridge, so the resulting floods must have been intense.

Although reaching the island is still possible, it is now accompanied by a new set of challenges. A makeshift bridge was constructed over Huckleberry Creek. However, given the flood's destruction of the original, sturdier bridge, the longevity of this new bridge is anybody's guess.

Island Lake itself has undergone a dramatic transformation. A significant drop in water levels, due to the collapse of a natural dam, has pushed the shoreline out by over 100 feet and left sediment and mud deposits that could hinder access to the island. While I trust the USFS to eventually intervene and make necessary repairs to the trail and the bridge, Island Lake may be forever altered.

If you are considering a trek to the island, I strongly advise checking the latest trail updates before setting out. Also, be sure to review the "It's Dangerous To Go Alone" section in the appendices of this book for essential safety tips. It was a twelve-hour round trip for me, with only a couple of five-minute breaks and no lunch. Because of the flooding, downed trees, washed-out bridge, and other uncertainties, it will now undoubtedly take several hours longer.

Before attempting that hike in the wilderness at 7,600 feet, consider a trial near the safety of your home. There's no rush —*nothing* was left behind. I made sure of it in 2020 and went back in 2021 to be extra thorough after deciding to write this book. The only things left to find now are memories.

For Whom the Bell Tolls

WHEN A SEARCHER ASKED Forrest whether the finder would know why the spot was special to him, Forrest replied, "Maybe." While this implies that one can surmise the reason with enough research, we will never know for sure with Forrest gone.

Within the treasure chest was a small glass olive jar with a printed copy of Forrest's autobiography. The autobiography was originally going to explain the location's significance to Forrest, but he deleted that part, saying it was too personal. While my research led me to three strong possibilities as to why the location was important to him, I do not have the right to speculate about those possibilities. That story was Forrest's to tell, and he chose not to tell it.

I will say that, in the same way that Forrest's stories can contain more than one hint, perhaps the location was special to Forrest for more than one reason.

Bells were a theme that Forrest used, both in his writings and in the form of physical bells. Forrest created wax models of bells that he signed, dated, and had cast into bronze. Some of the bells contained quotes:

- "Imagination is more important than knowlege"
- "God will forgive me, that's what he does."
- "If you should ever think of me a thousand years from now, please ring my bell so I will know."

Other bells had embellishments such as faces or frogs incorporated into the design. Some of the bells had "clankers" made from large copper nails taken from 17th-century Spanish galleons.

Decades earlier, Forrest used to run a bronze foundry, so making the wax models and having them cast into bronze was something he was familiar with. Forrest buried a number of his bells in places so random that he claimed he couldn't find them again if he wanted to. He said he was trying to cause a momentary excitement in some future millennium.

In addition to painting some 15,000 paintings, Forrest's good friend, Eric Sloane, wrote 50 books over 50 years (according to Forrest). Some of Eric's books include:

- *Once Upon a Time: The Way America Was*
- *Diary of an Early American Boy*
- *A Reverence for Wood*
- *The Sound of Bells*

The Sound of Bells is full of historical "bell wisdoms." "The faraway sound of a bell could be both forlorn and soul-stirring," Eric once said. Bells were used to communicate a wide variety of messages over long distances. Eric notes that death knells during a funeral were "two times three for a woman and three times three for a man." Recalling that passage, Forrest said that, "Eric liked to pick up an old bell in my office that rested on a banco near the fireplace, and thump it three times three."

My War for Me

The true poet has no choice of material. The material plainly chooses him, not he it.

J. D. Salinger

THE CHASE STARTED in 2010 for searchers. For Forrest, it had started over three decades earlier. *The Thrill of the Chase* was not some lark, and although there was a treasure patiently waiting for searchers to find, it was not a simple treasure hunt. Nor was it the single memoir of the same name. It was Forrest's magnum opus: the 24 verses of the poem that led to the treasure, all three of Forrest's memoirs, Seventeen Dollars a Square Inch, the scrapbooks, the interviews, the interaction with searchers, the game, and the story. It was promises kept.

Forrest once said, if you read nothing else, read the chapter, "My War For Me." My War For Me. Forrest's war. Forrest's war for himself. From my vantage point, way up in the cheap seats, "My War For Me" was not about the Vietnam War; it was about Forrest's War, and the stakes were high. I think he won.

PART IV
Appendices

It's Dangerous To Go Alone

FOR THOSE PLANNING to visit the general location, and, especially for those planning to visit the island, I feel compelled to offer a few safety tips:

1. Forrest said the area was safe. In my opinion, it is safe. But safe is subjective, and safe does not mean free from the possibility of harm. What's safe to me might not be safe to you. What I'm used to might not be what you're used to. I'm used to hiking all day with no food and sharing the woods with wildlife that might view me as food. If you are not used to hiking through the woods alone, do not pick this hike to start doing so. It's dangerous to go alone. Take a friend.
2. The section of the hike over the rock tailings and boulders is more technical, and those not used to that type of hiking may have a difficult time there. Loose dirt on a rock can be as slippery as water. Careful footing and ensuring that you are stepping on something solid before putting your weight down is always appropriate.

3. Trail conditions change year to year and sometimes day to day. There was a new boulder blocking part of the path in 2021 that was not there in 2020. If you go too early in the year, before the forest crews have had a chance to clear downed trees and debris, you might find the trails impassable. The trail you hike will not be the same trail that I hiked.
4. The area in question is grizzly country. Be prepared to see grizzlies. You probably won't, because they don't want to see you either. But just in case, be prepared. Don't put your faith in wearing bells; grizzlies treat bells as a call to dinner. If you are going around a blind corner, or anywhere else you cannot see, make human noises. Baby bears—typically guarded by mama bears—are extremely dangerous. Carry bear spray. If you see a grizzly 100 yards in the distance, get the bear spray ready. A grizzly can cover that distance in less than ten seconds. Many books have been written on bear safety, and I suggest you read one before heading out.
5. Don't go in winter. Don't go in spring. Don't go when there's snow on the ground. When I mentioned slippery rocks, it was not for effect. Moss-covered rocks are slippery. Wet rocks are slippery. Ice is slippery. Search for *"Mystic Lake Montana weather"* for current weather conditions. It rains there more than you might guess.
6. The area is in a box canyon, and it's almost impossible to get lost, especially if you stay on the trail. However, if you are bringing a phone to take pictures anyway, you might as well throw AllTrails, Gaia GPS, or some other good mapping software on there, just in case. Google Maps and Apple Maps do not qualify as good mapping software for this purpose.
7. The trail starts at 6,600 feet, climbs to 7,900 feet, and then drops down to 7,600 feet at the shore of the lake. That's not terribly high, but everyone is different. If you have lived on the coast all your life, the elevation

difference might cause problems. First, there's altitude sickness. This is unlikely, but again, everyone is different. If you think you might be susceptible, extend your trip and stay in camp for a few days before making a long hike. Second, there is less oxygen at that altitude. A hike along the coast is easier than a hike at 7,600 feet, no matter how good of shape you are in. I hike at 4,000 feet all the time, and I can tell the elevation difference.

8. If you plan to make the trip to the island, first make sure you can walk 14 miles in one day with whatever you'll be carrying on your back. If you cannot safely walk 14 miles at home, do not try hiking 14 miles in the wilderness at 7,600 feet. The trail incorporates a vertical climb of 1,000 feet over a one-mile stretch, so make sure your test hikes include that. If they don't, add some weight to your backpack or ankles to simulate it.
9. Look up the term "thru-hiking" for tips from experts at hiking long distances. Look for advice on how to approach a long hike, as well as tips on lightweight gear. Pay special attention to shoes. A good pair of hiking shoes can make all the difference.
10. Take a flashlight if you think there is a chance you won't be back before dark. I always have a flashlight in my backpack, even if I'm going for a morning hike.
11. Factor in the weight of enough food to get you there and back. Even if you can walk all day without eating, taking some emergency food is always a good idea. There is plenty of water available, but filter it before drinking. Bring a filter that allows you to fill a container rather than one that makes you drink through a straw. You will not always have access to a water source and should carry some water with you at all times.
12. If you plan to cross the sound to the island, make sure you can do so safely. I used an Alpacka Packraft, and I highly recommend them. There are a lot of questionable rafts on the market, so look for reviews before buying.

Watching a video of someone flailing around trying not to capsize might tell you why a particular raft sells for so much less than others. If you have never used a kayak, canoe, or packraft before, make sure your first use is not out in the wilderness. Also, be sure to take along a patch kit and know how to use it.

13. The hike from the Mystic Lake Trailhead to Island Lake, unpacking and readying my raft, rowing out to the island, exploring for a couple of hours, rowing back to the lake shore, packing the raft back up, and then hiking back to the trailhead took me approximately twelve hours. Everyone's experience can vary. Trying to make that trip without going on a fourteen-mile test hike first is irresponsible.

14. There is no cell phone reception, not in the campground nor in the surrounding areas. No one is out there to assist you. If you go in alone, you will be alone. That said, certain methods allow communication with the outside world in remote locales. The Garmin inReach and SPOT Satellite Messengers are two viable options. But even with such devices, rescue could still be hours or more away. Furthermore, electronics are susceptible to failure and drained batteries, particularly in cold conditions. Anticipate and prepare for such scenarios.

15. I highly recommend taking a Wilderness First Aid course from Wilderness Medical Associates (*wildmed.com*). First aid in the wilderness differs from first aid in civilization. In the wilderness, you can't count on an ambulance and a trip to a hospital. You have to assume that no one will be coming to help you and that you will have to improvise. The courses offered by Wildmed take that into account. If they do not provide a class near you, I suggest their *Wilderness and Rescue Medicine* textbook and their *Field Guide of Wilderness & Rescue Medicine*.

Anatomy of a Hint

THE REST of the appendices feature bonus content on the methods used to prospect for hints and clues. The examples were pulled from my aberrations notebook and cleaned up to make them more readable. They should be viewed as random ramblings—going nowhere and connected to nothing.

For every potential hint, I started my analysis by considering the possibility that what I was looking at was not a hint. That was always the first possibility. Maybe an aberration was a marketing tool that Forrest used. Alternatively, he might have repeated a phrase simply because he liked how it sounded. An aberration was just an aberration until proven otherwise.

If I was determined to investigate a potential hint, the first and most important thing I did was get myself into the correct frame of mind. I was not looking for *the* explanation for the newfound hint; I was looking for all possible explanations. No matter how silly they sounded, I wrote them down.

Thinking, "no, that's not it" could result in tossing away helpful information. There was always the possibility that Forrest hid a single hint through multiple aberrations and that no single decoded aberration would result in the answer. Piecing a hint together without all the pieces would be impossible. I couldn't risk throwing away a potential part of a puzzle just because an interpretation for that part did not make sense at the time it was discovered. Until I had the hint in hand, every explanation was viable.

There were nine clues in the poem, and a hint could apply to any of them. A hint could also apply to a general area, river, road, state, place name, or dozens of other possibilities, both known and unknown to me. It was critical not to hobble a hint by tying it to somewhere it did not belong, and I could not be sure where it belonged until after the solution was complete.

Another possibility worth considering was that a hint might not have anything to do with the location of the treasure chest—it might be pointing to the purpose of the game.

I found it helpful to explicitly justify to myself why I thought an aberration was a hint. For example, in *The Thrill of the Chase*, Forrest talked about hunting meadowlarks and scissortails for his family's dinner. Why might that be a hint? Because those birds are so small, they would not make more than a mouthful. I therefore viewed that story's hint-containing probability as high. One of the possibilities for that aberration was that the meadowlark is the state bird of both Montana and Wyoming. Was that a hint that narrowed the search to those two states? And what of scissortails?

Admittedly, I harbored one particular bias when analyzing potential hints. I always preferred subtle over unsubtle interpretations. I would rather have to work for the hint. I would make a note of the obvious interpretations, but I would keep looking.

Even though the chase has ended, I still make entries in my aberrations notebook. For example, take the "Montana Golden" story in *Once Upon a While*. In that story, Forrest said he hid a Dr Pepper under a rock in the lake to save for the next time he made that hike. Yet, in a document titled "Ramblings and Rumblings," written by Forrest before *The Thrill of the Chase* was released—and which I did not know about until six months after the chase had ended—this was a Coke, not a Dr Pepper. Adding this tidbit to my aberrations notebook made no difference, but my notebook would not be complete without it.

Yellowstone

WITH ALL OF Forrest's talk about Yellowstone, including a chapter in *The Thrill of the Chase* titled "In Love with Yellowstone," believing he hid the treasure chest there was not an unreasonable initial opinion. Forrest not only seemed to be shouting "Yellowstone!" from the rooftops, but he went out of his way to include subtle hints pointing in that direction as well. For example:

- In the "Sweet Fragrances" chapter of *Once Upon a While*, Forrest hinted at Yellowstone with the statement, "I felt jaundiced and had to suck on an ice cube." Jaundice and ice equate to yellow and stone, respectively.
- In a story titled "The Dragon Bracelet" that appeared on *DalNeitzel.com*, Forrest talks about trading a "43-carat…canary diamond" to Eric Sloane for a "Campbell Soup box full of money." One of the many things that stand out in that story is the "canary diamond." A canary diamond is a yellow diamond—a yellow stone.

The subtle hints at Yellowstone intrigued me. Why was Forrest giving subtle hints to Yellowstone when he included a chapter titled

"In Love with Yellowstone" within *The Thrill of the Chase*? Maybe these subtler hints were a way of saying, "Yes, I really am hinting at Yellowstone."

If Forrest *was* hinting at Yellowstone, what was the nature of the hints? It's almost automatic to think that a specific hint points to the treasure's hiding spot. But there were nine clues in the poem, and each one could have had associated hints. A prime example is that the hints could have been Forrest's way of trying to help people with the first clue. Forrest was consistent with his emphasis that "if you don't have the first clue, you don't have anything." If the first clue was that essential and Forrest wanted the poem to be solved, there is a good chance he would try to help people with that most critical clue.

Forrest could have also been hinting toward a broad section of the search area, and that section of the search area did not have to mean Yellowstone National Park. The hints could have been pointing toward the town of West Yellowstone, which is not in the park. Or maybe Forrest was just guiding searchers to the general area instead of New Mexico or Colorado. To Forrest, maybe "Yellowstone" did not mean Yellowstone Park as much as it meant the Greater Yellowstone Ecosystem. The title of the chapter is, after all, "In Love with Yellowstone," not "In Love with Yellowstone National Park." For example, did Forrest's memories, outlined within the chapter "Looking for Lewis and Clark," not shine quite as bright because that trip was outside the park? For someone as allergic to rules and borders as much as Forrest, this line of thinking made sense to me.

The Yellowstone hints presented even more possibilities, such as the Yellowstone River and Yellowstone Lake. I addressed these possibilities by refusing to dismiss any of them outright. Until I was holding a bronze chest in my hands, every possibility was still possible.

It's Not Easy Being Green

IN THE CHAPTER "Dancing with the Millennium" in *The Thrill of the Chase*, while talking about making bronze bells and jars, Forrest said, "Frogs are kind of my specialty because I like to fabricate long legs and buggy eyes in the soft wax." Forrest would decorate his bells and jars with embellishments like frogs, dragonflies, faces, and quotations.

Frogs were a puzzling minor theme, at least I thought so. Besides Forrest's fabricated frogs cast in bronze, there were two gold frogs included within the chest, one of which took center stage in many of the discussions about the chest contents. Maybe Forrest just liked frogs. That could be. But like every other oddity I noticed in Forrest's words, frogs eventually earned an entry in my aberrations notebook.

My research into Forrest's frogs brought up quite a few possibilities, some more interesting than others. Here are six:

1. They were just frogs.
2. One definition of frog is "A recess in a brick."
3. Another definition of frog is "An airplane designed to take off and land on both land and water."

4. The Rainbow Connection. The potential connection here is weak, but it makes me smile. In "Tea with Olga," Forrest talks about scattering his neighbor Olga's ashes near the top of Taos Mountain. Jim "Kermit" Henson's ashes were scattered near Taos Mountain as well. This is just a vague connection to a frog in a swamp on an island on the other side of a rainbow.
5. "I like to fabricate long legs and buggy eyes in the soft wax," said Forrest. From long legs to buggy eyes. Could Forrest have been hinting at long legs of a journey ending at a conspicuous eye? I cross-referenced this possibility in my notes to Forrest's frequent mentioning of Wimpy hamburgers and, through that reference, to Popeye.
6. Frog » Amphibian » Amphibiology » Amphibology » Amphiboly. I encourage you to explore the definitions of Amphibology and Amphiboly, then compare those meanings to the following statements from Forrest:

> *"One of my natural instincts is to embellish just a little."*
> *"I removed all the commas..."*
> *"I tend to bend word meanings..."*
> *"I make up words...."*
> *" I don't want to use anybody's book-writing rules."*
> *"Frogs are kind of my specialty because I like to fabricate..."*
>
> Forrest Fenn

Holes

IT SLIPPED my mind that I watched the movie "Holes" as part of my research. I guess I didn't find anything there. I watched it because of Forrest's often-quoted line, "How deep is a hole?"

"How deep is a hole?" Forrest gave this as a reply to certain questions, even if the question did not warrant this as a reply. It was seemingly a hint that Forrest wanted to interject into the conversation. "How deep is a hole?" It depends on the hole. Perhaps that was Forrest's point; it is an unanswerable question. How deep is the deepest hole? Start by defining "hole."

Forrest often talked of his favorite fishing holes. What is a fishing hole? It is a deep and still section of a stream, creek, or river, where the flow of water slows, and the fish do not have to struggle against the current.

A hole is also an opening through something: a window, a hollow place in a solid body or mass, a cavity, the excavated habitation of an animal, a place of solitary confinement, a dungeon, a cave, a cavern, or a portal. It was of interest to me how often Forrest used the word "portal."

A hole does not have to be deep. A hole in a piece of punched paper is as shallow as the paper is thin.

A hole is also a part of a golf course—the part from a tee to the hole corresponding to that tee. Forrest spoke a lot about golf. I think he even said somewhere that he would have been a professional golfer but for his lack of skill.

These two quotes by Forrest about golf holes piqued my interest because of their similarity:

"Today I made a birdie on the 4th hole. That never happened to me before." Scrapbook 222.

"I made a hole in one on the 4th hole with a 7 iron." Scrapbook 230.

Forrest Fenn

On a related note, if you count a lake as a hole—an overly deep and still section of a stream—Island Lake becomes the fourth "hole" on the journey down the river and up the creek to the treasure's resting location. Island Lake is preceded by Mystic Lake, West Rosebud Lake, and Emerald Lake. Lily Pad Lake (Reeves Lake) is north of West Rosebud Creek and not part of the stream.

Connecting these two ideas: a synonym for "bird" is "plane." A birdie on the 4th hole. A plane on the 4th hole?

Clark Gable

CLARK GABLE WAS A CURIOUS ABERRATION, bringing up a few interesting possibilities, one of which shows how easy it is to find potential connections. Clark Gable was an actor who starred in films from the 1920s through 1961. He died in 1960, and his last film, *The Misfits*, with Marilyn Monroe, was released in 1961.

The aberration lay in Forrest's claim that his two daughters, Zoe and Kelly, did not know who Clark Gable was. This story stands out because everyone I know in Forrest's daughters' age range knows who Clark Gable was. Everyone. Alhough I had never watched any of his films, even I had heard of him. Of course, Forrest's daughters knew who Clark Gable was. Thank you for the homework assignment, Forrest. To be fair to Forrest though, I am certain that at some point in their lives, Forrest's daughters truly did not know who Clark Gable was.

Because I bounced around a lot between research topics, I didn't delve very deeply into the Clark Gable aberration, so I probably missed something. Here are a few of the possibilities I came up with:

1. Forrest's story was true, and his daughters did not know who Clark Gable was.

2. Forrest's story was just an embellishment that added flavor and was of no significance.
3. When telling the Clark Gable story in interviews, Forrest usually followed up by telling a story about how his grandmother had watched Comanches chasing chickens in Fort Worth. Why were the two stories linked? It might be worth trying to find an explanation.
4. Clark Gable's full name was William Clark Gable. Was this a pointer to William Clark of the "Looking for Lewis and Clark" story in *The Thrill of the Chase*? Could this have been Forrest's way of telling searchers to pay attention to that chapter?
5. "Gable" translates to "Fork" in German. Could this point to the Clarks Fork of the Yellowstone River?

One curious possibility was a potential connection to "The City on the Edge of Forever." Remember that Forrest's daughter Kelly did not know who Clark Gable was. In the classic *Star Trek* episode, "The City on the Edge of Forever," Doctor McCoy, played by actor DeForrest Kelly, did not know who Clark Gable was.

"The City on the Edge of Forever" is a time-travel story that takes place in 1930, the year Forrest was born. McCoy goes crazy, loses his memory, jumps through a portal to the past, and Kirk and Spock jump through after him. The story is about time and how an event in the past can have ripples that echo into the future. Time is fluid, with currents, eddies, and backwash.

In the story, Kirk falls in love with the character Edith Keeler, played by Joan Collins. Spock discovers that Keeler had, in the unaltered timeline, died in 1930. McCoy had interfered with the past and prevented that death. Because Keeler lived, history was changed throughout the galaxy. Kirk must decide whether or not to prevent McCoy from saving Keeler. Kirk decides, Keeler dies, and history is restored.

There are many takeaways from this story, including that the choices one makes have lasting repercussions. Another speaks to the potential effect that a single person can have on history.

The Rosetta Stone

IN THE CHAPTER "ORDER FROM CHAOS," I made an offhand remark about the Rosetta Stone. Undoubtedly, non-searchers were left wondering what I was talking about. The Rosetta Stone was a topic that Forrest routinely brought up in interviews: "The Rosetta Stone was buried for 2,000 years before somebody found it, and I said in my book, 'Don't you know that guy is proud?' The guy that carved that Rosetta Stone."

In "Order from Chaos," I implied that the Rosetta Stone reference served as a hint pointing towards Booty Island of Island Lake. While I do not know that for certain, that's my best guess. Another possibility is that it is just a marketing line Forrest used for interviews. A more complex prospect is that Forrest is referring to a literal Rosetta Stone—a key to unlocking and translating his words. The actual Rosetta Stone contains three versions of the same text, all written in different languages. It was an essential key to understanding the Egyptian hieroglyphic script.

My methodology for solving the poem incorporated the idea that Forrest created his own language, Fennglish, to hide clues and hints. Forrest's continuous mentioning of the Rosetta Stone could be hinting that a translation of his words was needed or that searchers needed to learn another language—Fennglish.

If Forrest was referring to an analogous Rosetta Stone for his books and other writings, what form might that take? It would need to include the means to translate text from one language to another. If one of the languages were Fennglish, as I surmise, then English would be a likely candidate for the second language.

Forrest gave several of his stories a test run through the *Bozeman Daily Chronicle* newspaper in 2008 before including the stories in his memoirs. I won't go over the differences between the newspaper version and the version that appeared in the memoirs, but going over the differences should have been on every searcher's to-do list. Search for "Forrest Fenn" on *bozemandailychronicle.com*, and the following should appear:

1. "Boyhood Memories of West Yellowstone Long Ago," Published February 7, 2008. This story merges the following two stories: "The Totem Café Caper" from *The Thrill of the Chase* and "Buffalo Smoke" from *Too Far to Walk*.
2. "How 'The Dude' came to West Yellowstone." Published February 28, 2008. Compare with "The Dude" from *Too Far to Walk*.
3. "Memories of the past enrich our present." Published May 7, 2008. Compare to "Flywater" in *The Thrill of the Chase*.
4. "Looking for Lewis and Clark." Published May 27, 2008. Compare to the story of the same name in *The Thrill of the Chase*.

Forrest said that if you read anything of his, read "My War For Me" from *The Thrill of the Chase*. Like the stories above, My War For Me has been published elsewhere. In Scrapbook 138, Forrest recounts writing the story for the Super Sabre Society. It is unclear when the story first appeared on *supersabresociety.com*. The earliest I see is from 2020, but that's not right, as *The Thrill of the Chase* was published in 2010.

At the time of writing, "My War For Me" also appears on *85fis.doncondra.org*. That site says that the version of the story they host is from 2006, but the earliest version I see published there is from 2009. That version seems to be close to the version published in *The Thrill of the Chase*.

All of the stories that Forrest published before *The Thrill of the Chase* could be a type of Rosetta Stone for Forrest's words, whether Forrest intended them to be so or not. These were easy to find, and most searchers must have known about them.

There was another document floating about that was guarded like the crown jewels: *Ramblings and Rumblings*. If a Rosetta Stone existed for *The Thrill of the Chase*, it was *Ramblings and Rumblings*.

I found out about *Ramblings and Rumblings* when Dal Neitzel released it on his website after Forrest passed away. *R&R* appears to be an early draft of many of the stories that would later appear in Forrest's memoirs.

One notable example of *R&R* serving as a potential Rosetta Stone is a draft version of the chapter, "Montana Golden" from *Once Upon a While*. In the draft version of the story, Forrest traveled to Lost Lake, not Avalanche Lake. Forrest had to change that because there is no Lost Lake where he said the story took place. There is, however, a Lost Lake near the Avalanche Lake that sits between Granite Peak and Mystic Lake. Another notable piece of this puzzle is that this story, as told in *Ramblings and Rumblings*, is part of the "Looking for Lewis and Clark" story and directly links "the highest mountain they'd ever seen" to both Lost Lake and Avalanche Lake.

I saw Ramblings and Rumblings as a gold mine of information. R&R contains stories and parts of stories that have never appeared elsewhere. A lot of the stories that appeared in the memoirs were reworked considerably form the *R&R* version, indicating possible hints. Just to clarify, however, I am not saying this is the "Rosetta Stone" Forrest spoke of, but it did seem like a remote possibility.

Dizzy Dean

DIZZY DEAN WAS RENOWNED as a professional baseball pitcher. In the revised edition of Forrest's third memoir, *Once Upon a While*, a story about Dizzy Dean was notably introduced. This inclusion was significant as it was the sole fresh tale in the revised edition. In addition to the Dizzy Dean story, the updated edition featured a number of minor changes plus a few new doodles. The term "minor" should not be misconstrued as "trivial." "Why in the world did he go to the trouble to change that?" I would ask myself.

Like most of Forrest's stories, the tale of Dizzy Dean contained several potential hints. Here are a few:

1. Dizzy Dean's real name was Jay Hanna "Dizzy" Dean. This raises the faint possibility of hinting at Hanna, Wyoming. According to *hannabasinmuseum.com*, "The Union Pacific Coal Company's No. 4 mine lies directly under the town of Hanna." In the northeast portion of the town limits is the neighborhood of Elmo. St. Elmo's Fire came to mind. Within the neighborhood of Elmo is a street named Rosebud Lane. A blaze on the rosebud near the number 4 hole? I feel coated by a thin film of

confirmation bias for including this, but thought some might be interested.
2. Dr Pepper is mentioned a few times in the new Dizzy Dean story. Dr Pepper was a theme scattered throughout Forrest's writings, and I have several pages of notes about it. I've heard that visitors to Forrest's home would even be offered a frosty Dr Pepper as a refreshment.
3. The Dizzy Dean story first appeared as Scrapbook 188, which ends with, "I just read through my story above about Dizzy Dean, and removed all of the commas. I feel so good I may just go get myself another Dr Pepper." The thing about this that caught my eye, besides Dr Pepper, was the part about the commas. I thought it might be referring to either amphiboly (mentioned in another appendix) or Scrapbook 179.
4. Scrapbook 179 had an off-handed comment about Cormac McCarthy. You may be familiar with some of McCarthy's works, even if you aren't familiar with his name. "Cormac McCarthy was known to write a story and then go back and remove all of the commas," said Forrest. Was Forrest suggesting searchers ignore or play with punctuation? Maybe. Was there some work of Cormac McCarthy's that held a hint? Again, maybe. One of the notes I made at the time was that, during an interview, McCarthy said that he only respects authors who "deal with issues of life and death."

Another change that made searchers stand at attention was the addition of a lone omega symbol—Ω—on the last page of the revised edition. Searchers had speculated on the meaning of the omegas since the first year of the chase. Omegas were absent in the first edition of *Once Upon a While*, and then a single omega made an appearance in the revised edition. Surely Forrest knew what kind of commotion that would cause, but that did not stop him.

Forgotten

*

In another generation or so most of those names will be but an asterisk in the history of a forgotten war, a curiosity to wonder about.

The Thrill of the Chase

Those who fell there, in that hateful, wasteful, losing war (like the one in which I was involved) are forever forgotten, save by me. It has been fifty-six years since that war, and no one cries anymore.

The Thrill of the Chase

...to all the warped and broken wooden boards that lay lost and forgotten...

17 Dollars a Square Inch dedication

The ground knows and the tall grass knows, but they won't tell. And what of the wives and children of those soldiers? Have they gone on to live with a hundred forgotten memories?

The Thrill of the Chase

Did Shakespeare really say, in other words, that most of us come into this world for a little while, are blessed perhaps, then depart and are soon forgotten by history? Of course he did!

The Thrill of the Chase

I've never been willing to stand idly by and be part of a forgotten history when I may be able to impact future events.

The Thrill of the Chase

The painting was untitled, so I called it Forgotten.

Scrapbook 220

It languished, lost and forgotten, for almost 31 years.

Scrapbook 228

Look at me, I'm somebody; please don't forget.

The Thrill of the Chase

Bibliography

Below is a selection of works I consulted during my research. Each offered varying degrees of depth and usefulness.

Books

Baum, L. Frank. *The Wonderful Wizard of Oz*
    George M. Hill Company, 1900.

Burton, Gabrielle. *I'm Running Away from Home, But I'm Not Allowed to Cross the Street*, Know, Inc., 1972.

Carroll, Lewis. *Alice's Adventures in Wonderland*
    Macmillan, 1865.

Carroll, Lewis. *Through the Looking-Glass*
    Macmillan, 1871.

Fenn, Forrest. *Once Upon a While*
    Phat Page Design, 2017.

Fenn, Forrest. *Once Upon a While - Revised Edition*
   One Horse Land & Cattle Company, 2019.

Fenn, Forrest. *Seventeen Dollars a Square Inch*
   One Horse Land & Cattle Company, 2007.

Fenn, Forrest. *The Thrill of the Chase*
   One Horse Land & Cattle Company, 2010.

Fenn, Forrest. *Too Far to Walk*
   One Horse Land & Cattle Company, 2013.

Fitzgerald, F. Scott. *The Great Gatsby*
   Scribner, 1925.

Grey, Zane. *The Code of the West*
   Harper & Brothers, 1934.

Heinlein, Robert. *I Will Fear No Evil*
   Putnam, 1970.

Heinlein, Robert. *Stranger in a Strange Land*
   Putnam, 1961

Hemingway, Ernest. *A Farewell to Arms*
   Scribner, 1929.

Hemingway, Ernest. *For Whom the Bell Tolls*
   Scribner, 1940.

Khayyam, Omar. *Rubaiyat*
   Bernard Quaritch, 1859.

Knoblock, Edward. *Kismet*
   Walter H. Baker Company, 1922.

McClintock, Grant; Crockett, Mike. *Flywater*
   Globe Pequot Press, 1994.

Melville, Herman. *Mardi: And a Voyage Thither*
   Harper & Brothers, 1849.

Norris, P. W. *The Calumet of the Coteau*
   J. B. Lippincott & Co., 1884.

Parsons, James. *The Art Fever*
   Gallery West, Inc., 1981.

Poe, Edgar Allen. *The Goldbug*
   Philadelphia Dollar Newspaper, 1843.

Preston, Douglas. *The Codex*
   Tor Books, 2003

Preston, Douglas. *Two Graves*
   Grand Central Publishing, 2012.

Redford, Robert. *The Outlaw Trail: A Journey Through Time*
   Gosset & Dunlap, 1976.

Russell, Osborne. *Journal of a Trapper*
   Syms-York Company, 1921.
   This was the most readable version I could find that was edited from the original manuscript.

Salinger, J.D. *Catcher in the Rye*
   Little, Brown and Company, 1951.

Sloane, Eric. *A Reverence for Wood*
   Dover, 2004.

Sloane, Eric. *Camouflage Simplified*
   Devin-Adair, 1942.

Sloane, Eric. *Diary of an Early American Boy*
   Dover, 2004.

Sloane, Eric. *Eighty*
   Dodd, Mead & Company, 1985.

Stevenson, Robert Louis. *Treasure Island*
   Cassell and Company, 1883.

Strobridge, Idah Meacham. *The Loom of the Desert*
   Baumgardt, 1907.

Poems

Miscellaneous Poems:
   Clarke, Herbert Edwin. "In the Wood", 1852.
   Eliot, T. S. *Four Quartets*, 1941.
   Henley, William Ernest. "Invictus", 1888.
   Parker, Bonnie. "The Story of Suicide Sal", 1932.
   Poe, Edgar Allan. "Annabel Lee", 1849.
   Poe, Edgar Allan. "The Raven", 1845.
   Longfellow, Henry Wadsworth. "A Psalm of Life", 1838.
   Millay, Edna St. Vincent. *A Few Figs from Thistles*, 1920.
   Scott, Sir Walter. "The Lady of the Lake", 1810.
   Seeger, Alan. "I have a Rendezvous with Death", 1916.
   Yeats, W. B. "The Hour Glass", 1900.

Movies

Errol Flynn Movies:
  Adventures of Robin Hood, 1938
  Montana, 1950
  Rocky Mountain, 1950
  Santa Fe Trail, 1940
  The Sun Also Rises, 1957
  They Died With Their Boots On, 1941

Miscellaneous Movies:
  It's a Mad, Mad, Mad World, 1963
  Jewel of the Nile, 1985
  Lonesome Dove, 1985
  Lucky Luke, 1991, Narrated by Roger Miller
  National Treasure, 2004
  National Treasure 2, 2007
  Romancing the Stone, 1984
  The Ballad of Buster Scruggs, 2018
  The Book of Eli, 2010
  The Great Gatsby, 1974
  The Harvey Girls, 1946
  The Wizard of Oz, 1939
  To Catch a Thief, 1955

Television Episodes

Twilight Zone, Season 5, Episode 11
  "The 7th is Made Up of Phantoms"

Star Trek, The Original Series
  "City on the Edge of Forever"

Epilogue

IN THE PREFACE, I expressed skepticism about the solution and story being concealed. This does not mean I am criticizing the decision to keep everything secret. Had Forrest had asked me to keep his secrets, this book would not exist. If Forrest had said to the general public, "I don't want the solution known," this book would not exist. While writing *The Place Where a Story Ended*, I have re-examined a large percentage of Forrest's words, looking for a hint either way. If I had found anything that tipped the scales toward keeping everything a secret, this book would not exist. While I am skeptical of the reasons, I do not necessarily understand those reasons, and I may be missing something.

That being said, I have solid reasons for believing that Forrest wanted this story told—at least in the beginning—and can make a strong case for that opinion. This is not just Forrest's story. This is also the story of a young boy, Mark Edward Von Seggern. It is about how 300,000 people searched for him over ten years and how he has not been forgotten. This story deserves to be told, and if no one else will tell the tale, I will.

Could my solution to Forrest's poem be incorrect? My methodology says that I could be wrong, that no poem interpretation can receive a 100% score without a bronze chest in hand. Could there exist a different solution that fits the clues and hints as well as or better than the solution detailed in this book? Again, my methodology says that is a possibility. I think it would be fascinating if that turned out to be the case, but until I see that solution, my probability meter is trending toward "no."

If my solution is incorrect, it is irrelevant whether I release it. If my solution is correct, but there is a valid reason to deny it, I'm okay with that. But if my solution is right and this is Forrest's story, I not only don't see a problem with telling it, I see a problem with not telling it.

There are several verses in the poem not explained within this book. The missing pieces of Forrest's puzzle were omitted on purpose and for reasons already given. I never intended this book to be a "searcher's thesis" where I explain every little piece of the puzzle in detail. I wrote *The Place Where a Story Ended* to be readable by non-searchers, and putting them to sleep was not a goal. I don't know how well that worked out, but I do know that I stopped writing about a subject when the subject put me to sleep.

For those who do not believe the solution presented here, adding the missing pieces would not help. For those who do believe this solution, you should be able to work out the remaining mysteries on your own should you be so inclined.

Acknowledgments

I want to express my sincere gratitude to:

The Old Hag

Even though I locked myself away from the world, spent every spare waking moment buried in research, and kept putting off fixing the dishwasher as my wife had asked, she was still kind enough to support this endeavor. Early on, she volunteered to type up both *The Thrill of the Chase* and *Too Far to Walk* so I would have searchable copies. There are ways to automate that, but typing by hand can bring extra insight.

After transcribing Forrest's second memoir, she gave up on the chase, so I never got a searchable copy of the third. I tried bribing her with her favorite foods but had no luck. She was done. I blame Osborne Russell's book, *Journal of a Trapper*. I don't know how far she got into it before throwing it back at me, but I don't think more than halfway. It affected her. If you knew what I was using as a bribe, you would agree.

After checking out of the chase, she never checked back in. On occasion, when seeing me smile at some new morsel I had found, she would ask me how it was going. That was a courtesy question. If I could not make my point within thirty seconds, her spirit would leave her body and float to the next room, where she would work on some imaginary spreadsheet in her head.

Being of a scientific mind, I conducted experiments to see if I could measure the phenomenon. Paying close attention to her micro-expressions, I could tell within one second when my words started bouncing off the shell she had left behind. Thirty seconds was the longest I measured. When confronted with the evidence, she remarked that I sounded like a lower-pitched version of Charlie Brown's teacher—in a soothing and hypnotizing sort of way.

There were several occasions when she noticed essential confirmations that I had missed. One had to do with the elevation of Mystic Lake. When talking about the hike to the lake, I mentioned that the hike started at around 6,600 feet, climbed 1,300 feet, and then dropped down 300 feet to the shore of the lake.

"The lake is at 7,600 feet?" she asked.

"It varies, but thereabouts," I replied.

"7,600 feet?" she repeated.

"Yes," I confirmed.

She was staring at me now, unblinkingly, but this time, her spirit was not doing its usual dance into the other room. After a long pause, "The chest is located between 5,000 and 10,200 feet?" she asked with an emphasis that I noticed but ignored.

"That's what the man said."

There was another long pause. She was looking at me with disappointment in her eyes. Thankfully, she did not draw it out any longer, "7,600 is halfway between 5,000 and 10,200." My expression betrayed my attempt to act nonchalant.

One time my wife gave me homework which led to a confirmation. When talking with her about "Tea with Olga," I mentioned the aberration where Forrest implies that Taos Mountain was 90 miles from Santa Fe when it's not.

"Did you measure out 90 miles from Santa Fe in all directions to see if anything was there?" she inquired.

I gave her a look that answered her question.

"Both statute and nautical miles?" she shot back.

My look changed and let her know that I had homework. I eventually circled back and remeasured other distances Forrest mentioned concerning flying. That's when the 600 nautical miles to Mystic Lake emerged as part of the map's X.

Another confirmation she noticed was with *The Catcher in the Rye*. She immediately caught the connection after I told her the story of the accident at the top of the pass involving young Mark Edward Von Seggern. I had only read *The Catcher in the Rye* once by then, and the connection she found had not yet made it into my aberrations notebook. Up to that point, my research gave me about 70% confidence that the memorial plaque was the blaze. When she pointed out *The Catcher in the Rye* connection, my confidence shot up to 90%. The translation of "tarry scant with marvel gaze" sealed the deal.

My wife was also the only person I trusted to proofread this book before publication and not leak the contents. Most of these words have her approval, and any typos, questionable grammar, or odd phrases that do not seem to fit are the result of my disregarding her suggestions.

Finally, I would like to thank my wife for giving me the gift of an email box overflowing with criticisms for calling her an "old hag." This section was initially called "The Confidant." It was my wife's idea to change the title to "The Old Hag." I think she's still laughing about it. Go figure.

The Nascent Beings

To those who introduced me to the chase, thank you for that initial email. These two rapscallions first heard about *The Thrill of the Chase* in the summer of 2018 through an episode of *Expedition Unknown*, so I suppose Josh Gates deserves some thanks as well.

The main culprit was so busy trying to figure out the arrow of time so she could build her own personal Tardis that she did not have any time left over to work on the chase. I am still counting on her, however, after which I expect a ride back in time. I have the coordinates right here.

Her cohort is an anthropologist at heart. After the chase was over, I thought we might take a road trip down to Santa Fe and talk to one of the locals who was heavily into that sort of thing. I heard he had connections to a dig site south of town and thought the two of them would have a lot to talk about. That trip has passed its due date, but maybe we'll figure something else out.

The Aide-de-Camp

Dal Neitzel, a friend of Forrest's, ran *DalNeitzel.com*, which stood out as the single greatest resource for searchers after Forrest himself. I used to have a gig running and moderating a website, and it's often a tiring and thankless job. That Dal was able to keep it up for so long is mind-boggling.

I had seen Dal's website early on, but I thought it was just another random treasure-hunting blog. One time, I was sent a link to a story on Dal's website, a 'scrapbook'. The story was written by someone pretending to be Forrest; they even signed the story with Forrest's trademark "f." The nerve of that guy Dal—allowing that nonsense on his site! I almost emailed Forrest about that. Little did I know, but that was where the big fish chose to swim. I'll always wonder if it would have helped or hurt had I understood what was going on over at Dal's place sooner.

Besides his website, Dal produced several interview series with Forrest. Dal's day job must have prepared him for the task, because those are the most professionally produced interviews of Forrest that exist. I watched all of Dal's videos that I could find but did not realize it was Dal who had shot them. I just thought it was some kind soul from a place called LummiFilm who decided to do the search community a favor.

I particularly liked the intensity with which Forrest approached favored subjects like artifacts from Sal Lazaro Pueblo or even just an old pile of broken pottery shards. Forrest's reverential descriptions of his old book collection are another favorite.

Dal's videos helped in figuring out who Forrest was beyond *The Thrill of the Chase*. I'm not sure how successful I was at that. Knowing the man behind the chase and getting a sense of how he spoke in general conversation helped determine when Forrest was joking around and when he was giving a hint. Again, I'm not sure how successful I was at that.

Check out Dal at *www.LummiFilm.com*. If you want to get to know Forrest, watch Dal's LummiFilm videos on the YouTube channel, "The Thrill of the Chase."

The Fourth Estate

Thanks to Jenny Kile over at *MysteriousWritings.com*. Jenny's treasure-hunting blog is one of only two I trusted for accurate and unembellished information from and about Forrest. If you are interested in treasure-hunting, check out *MysteriousWritings.com*.

Thanks to Lorene Mills for her many interviews with Forrest. Thanks to Toby Younis and Shelley Carney, whose Youtube channel was on the must-watch list for every serious searcher. Thanks to Richard Eeds for his radio interviews with Forrest. Thanks to Gadi Schwartz for being one of the early adopters and publishing articles about the chase. Thanks to Jason Dent for releasing the Playboy recording. Thanks to Cynthia Meachum for her behind-the-scenes videos with Forrest. And thanks to everyone else who published interviews with Forrest. The opportunity to directly connect with Forrest while the chase was in progress must be a treasured memory. Thank you for sharing those interviews with the world.

The Man from Temple

Thank you, Forrest, for the most fun I've had in the past 20 years. I wanted to meet you, shake your hand, and talk for a while, but I felt like I had to earn the right, and I didn't do that. So I'll settle for this virtual meeting and pretend that you have both read this book and are maybe smiling a bit right now.

Forrest was much more than an "eccentric art dealer" who hid a bronze chest full of gold and jewels in the mountains and then dared people to find it. The stories in his memoirs would make a good study guide to the way America was—once upon a time.

Forrest was born in 1930 and spent his first twenty years between Temple, Texas, and Yellowstone, with occasional excursions to other parts of the country.

Forrest never seemed to be out of a job and was willing to do just about anything—except for studying in school. He worked jobs doing whatever caught his interest and paid enough to buy an occasional Coke and a bag of Fritos, including: dishwasher, milk truck delivery boy, lumberjack, tying flies for a fly-fishing shop, and a fishing guide. Forrest got his entrepreneurial feet wet early on, making and selling marbles and yo-yos to the kids in his school.

Forrest had a self-deprecating sense of humor regarding his academic ability, saying, "I prayed for Ds in high school, but nobody ever listened," and that the reason he graduated was that his father was the school principal. Despite Forrest's downplaying of his schooling, there is evidence that he may have been debellishing his abilities in that arena. "Sounding stupid is a ploy I have used many times with great effectiveness," Forrest once said. This statement gave another meaning to Forrest's quote, "It's not who you are, it's who they think you are."

Forrest met his wife, Peggy, at age 15. Forrest was visiting his brother, Skippy, in the hospital after Skippy had been "blown up" in a firework stand accident. Skippy's girlfriend, Irene, stopped by for a visit and brought along her cousin, Peggy. Skippy married Irene and, eight years after the accident, Forrest married Peggy. They were married for 66 years.

Forrest enlisted in the Air Force in 1950, worked his way into pilot training a couple of years later, graduated from pilot training in 1953, and became Aide-de-Camp to Major General Frank Robinson in 1954. After training fighter pilots during the 1960s, Major Fenn volunteered to go to Vietnam. In Vietnam, Forrest was in charge of the command post at the Tuy Hoa Air Base. During his tour of duty, Forrest flew 328 missions in 348 days and was shot down twice. Forrest returned home on December 24, 1968.

By 1970, Forrest had a little bronze foundry in Lubbock, Texas, where he made bronze reproductions in his spare time. Forrest was offered a promotion to Colonel, but accepting it meant staying in the Air Force another two years. With his bronze foundry doing well, Forrest turned down the promotion to Colonel and retired from the Air Force with a Silver Star, a Bronze Star, three Distinguished Flying Crosses, fourteen Air Medals, and a Purple Heart.

Forrest moved to Santa Fe in 1972 and started the Fenn Galleries. For the next seventeen years, give or take, Forrest grew Fenn Galleries into one of the most successful art galleries in Santa

Fe. Many high-profile clients stayed at the gallery's guest house, including presidents, first ladies, and celebrities. Forrest's guest book, complete with personalized doodles from each guest, would be an autograph collector's dream come true.

Forrest transitioned from art dealer to archeologist when he purchased San Lazaro Pueblo, south of Santa Fe. The Tano Indians settled there in the 13th century and lived there until the Pueblo Revolt in 1680. Forrest estimates he excavated one percent of the pueblo or fifty of the five thousand rooms. Forrest would call in professional archeologists when he found something especially interesting or unusual, like when he found kachina dance masks, which were not supposed to exist in that area during that period.

Along with friend Mike Kammerer, Forrest sponsored an outreach program for troubled teens. Every year, they would bus a group of kids down from Wyoming to camp at San Lazaro Pueblo and teach them about archeology, San Lazaro and the people who lived there, the history of the region, and the disciplines of life.

Forrest said he never particularly cared for art; it was just a business to him. You can see this when comparing how Forrest talked about art with how he spoke of San Lazaro Pueblo and archeology. Forrest could talk for hours about an old pile of broken pottery shards. He could give the history of each one, when it was made, what it was used for, the meanings of the designs, and how the people of the time made pigments for the designs out of Rocky Mountain Beeweed.

From the age of nine, when he found his first arrowhead (was "an arrowhead at 9" a hint?), archeology was a theme that ran through the entirety of Forrest's life. Like fishing, it was not subject to his "don't do anything for more than 15 years" rule. Forrest had an academic interest in art; he had a passion for archeology.

Forrest wrote and published twelve books from 1980 through 2019:

The African Animals of W.R. Leigh with Sketches by William Robinson Leigh
    Fenn Galleries Publishing, 1980

The Beat of the Drum and the Whoop of the Dance
    Fenn Galleries Publishing, 1983

The Genius of Nicolai Fechin
    Nedra Matteuuci Galleries, 2001

The Secrets of San Lazaro Pueblo
    One Horse Land and Cattle Co., 2004

Historic American Indian Dolls
    One Horse Land and Cattle Co., 2007

Teepee Smoke: A New Look Into the Life and Work of Joseph Henry Sharp
    One Horse Land and Cattle Co., 2007

Seventeen Dollars a Square Inch
    One Horse Land and Cattle Co., 2007

The Thrill of the Chase
    One Horse Land and Cattle Co., 2010

Too Far to Walk
    One Horse Land and Cattle Co., 2013

Once Upon a While and *Once Upon a While - Revised Edition*
    Phat Page Design, 2017
    One Horse Land & Cattle Company, 2019

Leon Gaspard: The Call of Distant Places
    With Carleen Milburn, The Tia Collection, 2019

Educating Ardi
    Privately published, 2019

Forrest's roots ran deep.

Artwork

Cover Art:
   Photo by iStock.com/shin001.

Map Design:
   Compass Rose by Freedo, from openclipart.com.
   Feetprint by Vecteezy.com.
   Kayak by macrovector / Freepik.
   Mountains and paper background by blog.spoongraphics.co.uk.

Suggested Reading

Forrest's first memoir, *The Thrill of the Chase*, is distributed exclusively by Collected Works Bookstore in Santa Fe, New Mexico. That's the bible of the chase and, even though someone has already found the treasure chest, Forrest's memoirs are still worth reading.

Too Far to Walk and *Once Upon a While*, Forrest's second and third memoirs, can be obtained from either Collected Works Bookstore or <u>OldSantaFeTradingCo.com</u>. Most of Forrest's other books, including *Seventeen Dollars a Square Inch*, can also be obtained from <u>OldSantaFeTradingCo.com</u>.

By all accounts, *Chasing the Thrill*, by Daniel Barbarisi, is a worthy look into the universe that grew around Forrest Fenn's *The Thrill of the Chase*. While I haven't read it myself, I have heard enough good reviews to include it here.

When I am working on a problem, I never think about beauty. But when I have finished, if the solution is not beautiful, I know it is wrong.

Buckminster Fuller

About the Author

Hamice is the author of *The Place Where a Story Ended*. He has written a few works of a technical nature, but nothing that anyone has ever read. Hamice was just a surly curmudgeon, sailing o'er life's solemn main, when he found the footprints of another, and seeing, took heart again.

Hamice can be reached at *hcadae@gmail.com*, but take note that he only checks his email messages once or twice a week, and he will not be filling in any of the blanks.

www.ingramcontent.com/pod-product-compliance
Lightning Source LLC
Chambersburg PA
CBHW031144020426
42333CB00013B/499